Impacting
the Seven
Mountains

FROM THE

COURTS OF HEAVEN

Destiny Image Books by Robert Henderson

365 Prayers and Activations for Entering the Courts of Heaven

Unlocking Wealth from the Courts of Heaven

Resetting Economies from the Courts of Heaven
(mini-book)

Breaking the Stronghold of Iniquity
(with Bill Dennington)

Petitioning the Courts of Heaven During Times of Crisis
(mini-book)

Operating in the Courts of Heaven

Show Us Your Glory

Praying for the Prophetic Destiny of the United States and the Presidency of Donald J. Trump from the Courts of Heaven

Father, Friend, and Judge

Issuing Divine Restraining Orders from Courts of Heaven
(with Dr. Francis Myles)

Redeeming Your Bloodline
(with Hrvoje Sirovina)

The Cloud of Witnesses in the Courts of Heaven

Prayers and Declarations that Open the Courts of Heaven

Receiving Healing from the Courts of Heaven, Curriculum

Accessing the Courts of Heaven

Unlocking Destinies from the Courts of Heaven, Curriculum

Receiving Generational Blessings from the Courts of Heaven

Receiving Mantles from the Courts of Heaven

Impacting the Seven Mountains

from the Courts of Heaven

Kingdom Strategies for
Revival in the Church and
the Reformation of Culture

Robert Henderson

DESTINY IMAGE® PUBLISHERS, INC.
P.O. Box 310, Shippensburg, PA 17257-0310
"Promoting Inspired Lives."

This book and all other Destiny Image and Destiny Image Fiction books are available at Christian bookstores and distributors worldwide.

For more information on foreign distributors, call 717-532-3040.

Reach us on the Internet: www.destinyimage.com.

ISBN 13 TP: 978-0-7684-6271-5

ISBN 13 eBook: 978-0-7684-6272-2

ISBN 13 HC: 978-0-7684-6274-6

ISBN 13 LP: 978-0-7684-6273-9

For Worldwide Distribution, Printed in the U.S.A.

1 2 3 4 5 6 7 8 / 27 26 25 24 23

CONTENTS

INTRODUCTION

In today's world, there is so much chaos and upheaval. Viruses, political scandal, lies, fake news, and so many other issues are at work that it seems society is unraveling and disintegrating. The media's report is so skewed that it is virtually impossible to know when truth is being reported or when it is an outright lie. In the midst of this, however, God is still ruling and reigning from His position and Throne. He is not nervous nor uncertain about the outcome. He knows and is sure that His purposes will prevail. This will happen through the church that He initiated into the world. Hebrews 10:12-13 lets us know that Jesus' work on the cross and resurrection has set in motion the redeeming of all things back to Him and His purposes.

> But this Man, after He had offered one sacrifice for sins forever, sat down at the right hand of God, from that time waiting till His enemies are made His footstool.

Every enemy that is resisting or contrary to the will of God in the earth will become the footstool of the Lord Jesus Christ. In other words, it will be subdued under His authority and made to line up with His will. Notice that He is *waiting* for this to be brought into full manifestation. This implies that the church, which is the revelation of His body in the earth, is responsible for seeing these enemies brought under His rulership. We are here to subject all enemies under the power of His Lordship through the authority He has delegated to us.

Today, a great movement is occurring that is gaining tremendous momentum in connection to this. It is the whole idea of social reformation. In other words, the reclaiming of society that we have tended in years gone by to give away into the hands of the devil, which has led to our present circumstances. Because of our negligence, we now have much ground to make up and a time of recovery to enter. But I believe that the word of the Lord to us is the same as to David when he returned to Ziklag to find his encampment raided and everyone's wives, children, and possessions taken captive by an enemy. In I Samuel 30:8, we find David asking the Lord if he should go after that which had been captured and had therefore brought such despair and trouble to his whole army and to himself. The word of the Lord came to him saying that he should pursue, for he would recover everything:

> *So David inquired of the Lord, saying, "Shall I pursue this troop? Shall I overtake them?" And He answered him, "Pursue, for you shall surely overtake them and without fail recover all."*

I believe that as we pursue this whole concept of social reformation and invade what has been called the seven mountains of society, we will recover all without fail. We are not doing this out of our own power and might, but out of the supernatural power of God. We need to be faithful and diligent, and we need to be are aware that without the intervention of the Lord we will fail. We also know that if we are building what the Lord is building, we will be successful. Psalm 127:1 tells us that without the Lord's help, it is vain to build and even to stay awake and watch.

> *Unless the Lord builds the house,*
> *They labor in vain who build it;*
> *Unless the Lord guards the city,*
> *The watchman stays awake in vain.*

When we build what God is building and watch what God is protecting, we will be successful and fruitful in our endeavors. We will see the plan of God materialize in planet Earth. We have a confidence that we are laboring together with Him.

In the midst of the seven mountain mandate being espoused, there has been much talk about the reforming, redeeming, and reclaiming of these mountains. The seven mountains of religion, family, business, government, arts and entertainment, media, and education are the molders of society and the influencers of culture. If we are to see the kingdom of God manifest in the earth in a practical and revealed way, these structures and spheres must be penetrated and invaded with reformers.

This idea was first presented by Bill Bright of Campus Crusade and Loren Cunningham of Youth with a Mission (YWAM) fame. A few decades later, Lance Wallnau picked up on this revelation and took it to its present levels of influence and understanding. The invasion of these mountains and the altering of culture as a result is the *ultimate* manifestation of the kingdom of God in the earth. When Jesus came to the planet, He came preaching the gospel of the kingdom of God or the redemption of everything back to the sovereign rule of God. This was and is the agenda of our king—King Jesus. This job falls to the church that Jesus died to birth and form. It is the commissioned vehicle through which the Lord will invade these spheres that are referred to as mountains and begin to establish the rule of His government, kingdom, and authority in each. As this occurs, each of these mountains will begin

to take on the splendor of our Lord, Savior, and King—
Jesus. The Lord is busy impregnating His people with
a passion and jealousy to see all that is rightfully His
returned and restored to His rule.

We are awakening to the fact that everything in His
creation is to be under His authority. We have always
believed this, but we just thought that if we could hang
on and wait for Him to come back, He would accomplish it all at His physical return. We have realized now
that this isn't true. He will *finish* the task at His return,
but we have a role to play prior to that wonderful day.
This *finishing* is different from the finishing that Jesus
did on the cross when He uttered the words, "It is finished." By speaking those words, Jesus declared that
everything necessary to purchase back the creation of
God had now been accomplished. This statement from
the cross declared every legal mandate now in place
for God's will to be done in the earth. This includes the
reformations of society and culture. We must realize,
though, that the purchasing of something and the pos-
sessing of it are two very different things. Jesus paid
the price for all things to be redeemed back to God at
His death on the cross, but it is the job of the church to
possess what Jesus has now purchased including people, the earth, and all its societies.

First Corinthians 15:22-26 tells us that the last enemy
that will be defeated is death. We know that death will

be completely and totally abolished at the resurrection of the dead:

> *For as in Adam all die, even so in Christ all shall be made alive. But each one in his own order: Christ the firstfruits, afterward those who are Christ's at His coming. Then comes the end, when He delivers the kingdom to God the Father, when He puts an end to all rule and all authority and power. For He must reign till He has put all enemies under His feet. The last enemy that will be destroyed is death.*

It doesn't matter what eschatological view one holds—Jesus' return is the moment when death is destroyed and the dead come forth from their graves. If Jesus is returning to destroy the "last enemy," which is death, then that means every other enemy against the kingdom purposes of God in the earth is our responsibility. The cross of Jesus purchased our salvation to get us to heaven and bought the redemption of all of creation from the bondage it is in. We must not forfeit the greatness of the work of the cross and the resurrection by putting limits on its effect. Jesus' death, burial, and resurrection *bought back legally* all of the creation of God and its cultures and societies. It is the job of the church, God's people, to put fully and completely into place the victories that His glorious cross has purchased. This is where the reformation of society occurs as the seven mountains and molders of society are penetrated. This is our job as His kingdom people.

The purpose of this book is to seek to describe what each mountain would potentially look like when it is reformed. The reason is three-fold. We must be able to communicate in an effective way if we are to create visions in the heart of God's people. Without a passionate view of our purpose here on earth that establishes vision in our heart, we will never arise and go after it. Habakkuk 2:2 tells us that the vision must be written out in a plain way so that we can *run* with it:

> *Then the Lord answered me and said:*
> *"Write the vision*
> *And make it plain on tablets,*
> *That he may run who reads it."*

To run with a vision means that there is clarity so that without restraint we know what we are going after. We can *run* until we see the reality of it materialize. As a people, we must have this so that we can strive after the passion of God in the earth. When we begin to see what each individual mountain will look like reformed, we will have the vision that propels us on. It will be something that we will not only possess in our hearts, but it will possess us as well. When this occurs, we will be willing to lay down our lives for the fulfillment of God's plan in the earth.

Second, prayer points are needed in which we, the people of God, may engage ourselves. If we are to reform these influencers of culture referred to as mountains, we must win the victories first in the spirit realm. There are definite spiritual forces and principalities that are presently ruling these spheres. These victories must be won in the *Courts of Heaven.* Only as we take these powers to the Courts of Heaven can they be dismantled and lose the right to function. Evil powers can only control the mountains of influence because they claim a legal right to do this. We will discuss how to revoke and annul these claims so that these mountains might be reclaimed for the glory and purposes of the Lord.

If we are to penetrate and reform these mountains, we must recognize what these forces are and deal with them through apostolic intercession and decrees from the Courts of Heaven. We must also know how to call into being things that may not presently exist out of the spiritual dimension (see Romans 4:17). We can only do this if we can first *see* what the mountain should look like in a reformed state. As we realize and recognize the intentions of the Lord in these mountains, intercessors can be empowered to take their stand with boldness until what we have seen becomes a reality.

The final reason is to empower the raising up of reformers. Every believer is called to *one* of these mountains. This is their *kingdom purpose.* Each believer in the body of Christ should be equipped and empowered for this call, which is their heavenly agenda. Again, without a clear view of what a mountain in a reformed state should look like, how can we know what kind of reformers are to be produced? It will take the right kind of reformer to create the right kind of mountain so we get the right effects in society. One of the greatest challenges facing the body of Christ is producing the reformers are necessary to see these mountains reclaimed. When vision is created — when intercessors are empowered and reformers are produced and commissioned into their function in these mountains — we will see a living demonstration of the kingdom of God in planet earth through reformation. My definition of reformation is the tangible expression of the kingdom of God in society. This is what we are going after, believing for, and pushing toward. By God's grace, power, and His strategies unfolded, we will live to see the fullness of reformation of society realized in the earth. It is our Lord's passion and should be ours as well. I hope this book helps in this noble and high pursuit that we are after in the name of our Lord Jesus. Let us not stop until the job is complete and finished.

CHAPTER 1

THE SEVEN MOUNTAINS
AND THE KINGDOM OF GOD

The seven mountains, the molders of society and culture, must all be taken and brought into the order of God. We can then see a redeeming of society. Each one of these mountains must be reformed as an individual entity. As each mountain is reformed, then there will be a demonstration of redemption and reformation of the whole of the seven mountains. I want to peer into what this would look like when an entire social structure is reformed. My blueprint for this will be the word of God. The Lord does give us at least glimpses of what His ultimate intent in the earth looks like.

In order for the Lord's vision for society to come into reality, we need to make a distinction between the terms *society* and *culture*. The word *society* is defined as "the community of people living in a particular country or region and having shared customs, laws, and organizations." In other words, a society is a group or groups of people bound together by the dictates of living in the same geographical region, area, or territory. *Culture,* on the other hand, is defined as "the customs, institutions, and achievements of a particular nation, people, or group." So cultures exist within societies.

There are many different cultures within the American society. There is the Black culture, the Hispanic culture, the White culture, the Asian culture, the church culture, culture within business, and many other expressions within the whole of society. There can be nothing inherently wrong with any of these cultures. Each of these people groups called cultures have their own traditions, ways of doing things, ideas, and living structures. One culture is not better than another culture. We must give room for differing cultures and their way of doing things when they do not oppress another group of people or oppose the ways of God. Together, all of these cultures make up the society we live in. However, cultures must ultimately be submitted to the society they are a part of. For example, no one culture in America has a right to ignore the laws of our nation and have their own laws. This creates anarchy. Islam cannot introduce and live by Sharia law in America, when it is in contradiction to our federal, state, or local laws. In this instance, Muslims in the nation of America as a culture must abide by the laws of the society of America. This simple concept is trying to be ignored and dismissed. However, both society and the cultures that make up the society are to be reformed. They both can be an expression of the kingdom of God.

In actuality, *culture* would be considered *nations* as defined in the Bible. For instance, we are told in Matthew 28:19 that we are to make disciples of nations.

> *Go therefore and make disciples of all the nations,*
> *baptizing them in the name of the Father and of*
> *the Son and of the Holy Spirit.*

The word *nations* is the Greek word *ethnos*. It means "a race, tribe, as of the same habit." It is a culture. There are some who would contend that we are not called to affect political nations, only people groups with the same customs. However, this is ludicrous. This attitude creates vacuums that allow satanic strongholds to be built in governmental structures that rule countries. We are told in I Timothy 3:15 that the church is the pillar and ground of truth in society.

> *But if I am delayed, I write so that you may know*
> *how you ought to conduct yourself in the house*
> *of God, which is the church of the living God, the*
> *pillar and ground of the truth.*

The church is responsible to setting the standard of God in society and the cultures that make up these societies. We are to be discipling both of these. However, we are seeking to establish the *culture of the kingdom of God* within different cultures and societies. In other words, we desire to see the influence of the kingdom of God transform cultures/societies where they might be in conflict with God and His ways. This can be manifested in varying ways, as the kingdom of God prevails within the earth.

It is a society and its cultures that must be transformed and reformed. Our target is cultures/nations and their societies. These become affected as the kingdom impacts lives and society as a whole. The seven mountains are the molders of society. They mold the laws every culture lives under from the government mountain. They sometimes mold the oppression of certain cultures into poverty from the business mountain. They mold the cultural beliefs in our society from the media mountain. We could walk through every mountain, but my point is that these mountains fashion the mindsets, viewpoints, and lifestyles within our multi-cultured society. If we are going to free the cultures that constitute society, the seven mountains must be reformed and reclaimed for the kingdom of God.

So what would a society reformed as a whole look like? If we pictured it, how would it be framed? When someone takes a picture, to ensure that it is clear and in focus, the subject must be brought into *frame*. Otherwise, we cut someone or something out of the picture. Let's see if we can get *framed* and *focused* on what a picture of reformed society would look like in the western world.

We have heard powerful testimonies of what transformation looks like in third world countries where cities and regions have been dramatically impacted by the kingdom of God. These are agricultural regions for the most part, and we have heard the glowing reports of the prosperity that came through the harvest of their crops, the reduction of crime to almost non-existent, the peace that possessed the region, and the spiritual revival that occurred. These transformations are wonderful and should be applauded and celebrated. We need to evaluate them for what can be learned. But what does transformation and reformation look like in the western world where business people dress up and go to work in rush hour traffic? What does reformation look like where soccer moms drive children all over creation every day of the week? What does reformation look like when our children are faced with and have to combat the temptations of drugs, sex, and immorality at almost every turn? These are the questions that need to be considered and given some kind of answer. So what about it? What does the reformation of society look like? Let's take a look and picture reformation.

Scripture gives us many pictures of reformation in society. The Babylonian Empire in the days of Daniel is one of the first that comes to mind. When Nebuchadnezzar invaded and destroyed Israel and then carried away thousands of Jews back to his land, Babylon was a very heathen society. They were complete and total idol worshipers. They knew nothing or at least very little of the God of the Jews, Jehovah. But through the influence of Daniel and the others who were with him, Nebuchadnezzar acknowledged the God of Daniel and the Jews and even appears to have begun to worship and honor Him. Nebuchadnezzar went from a king who made idols to one who acknowledged and worshiped Jehovah, it appears, as his God.

Scripture describes how Nebuchadnezzar demanded that the image of gold that he had created be worshiped with no exceptions. Daniel 3:4-6 tells us that whoever would not worship that which the king had erected would be destroyed and killed:

> *Then a herald cried aloud: "To you it is commanded, O peoples, nations, and languages, that at the time you hear the sound of the horn, flute, harp, lyre, and psaltery, in symphony with all kinds of music, you shall fall down and worship*

> *the gold image that King Nebuchadnezzar has set up; and whoever does not fall down and worship shall be cast immediately into the midst of a burning fiery furnace."*

We know that the three Hebrew children known as Shadrach, Meshach, and Abed-Nego refused to do so and God came to their rescue. The point I want us to see here is how corrupt and idolatrous this whole nation was from the head down. But through encounter after encounter, we see King Nebuchadnezzar go from this place of great idolatry to the worship of Jehovah. Daniel 3:29-30 tells us that because of the faithfulness of Shadrach, Meshach, and Abed-Nego, God saved them, they were promoted in the kingdom of Babylon, and the king himself spoke favorably toward Jehovah:

> *"Therefore I make a decree that any people, nation, or language which speaks anything amiss against the God of Shadrach, Meshach, and Abed-Nego shall be cut in pieces, and their houses shall be made an ash heap; because there is no other God who can deliver like this." Then the king promoted Shadrach, Meshach, and Abed-Nego in the province of Babylon.*

The Lord also dealt severely with Nebuchadnezzar when he refused to humble himself. Because of his arrogance and pride, God allowed his mental capabilities to leave him for a season and then allowed them to return. After this affair, it appears that Nebuchadnezzar turned himself wholly to the Lord. Daniel 4:36-37 tells us:

> *At the same time my reason returned to me, and for the glory of my kingdom, my honor and splendor returned to me. My counselors and nobles resorted to me, I was restored to my kingdom, and excellent majesty was added to me. Now I, Nebuchadnezzar, praise and extol and honor the King of heaven, all of whose works are truth, and His ways justice. And those who walk in pride He is able to put down.*

Nebuchadnezzar is said to have honored, extolled, and worshiped the one true God. These things all happened through the influence of reformers such as Daniel, Shadrach, Meshach, and Abed-Nego. The kingdoms of Nebuchadnezzar and of Darius and Cyrus who followed were greatly affected by these men.

One of the chief reasons for the reformation of the highest places of this society was the prophecy of Jeremiah before the people of God went into Babylonian captivity. Jeremiah had exhorted the people prophetically not to approach their stay in Babylon with a temporary mindset, but to really put their feet down and have a reformer's effect. Jeremiah 29:4-7 tells us that the people of God were to infiltrate the society of Babylon and make it their land:

> *Thus says the Lord of hosts, the God of Israel, to all who were carried away captive, whom I have caused to be carried away from Jerusalem to Babylon:*
>
> *Build houses and dwell in them; plant gardens and eat their fruit. Take wives and beget sons and daughters; and take wives for your sons and give your daughters to husbands, so that they may bear sons and daughters – that you may be increased there, and not diminished. And seek the peace of the city where I have caused you to be carried away captive, and pray to the Lord for it; for in its peace you will have peace.*

Because those who went into captivity did so with a mindset that they were on a mission from God during this seventy-year period, Babylon became affected and infected with a kingdom people called the Jews. Notice what God commanded them to do while in Babylon. Again, first and foremost they were not to have a temporary mindset. They were not to be deceived that they were only going to be there a short period of time. God wanted them to know this was going to be their life for a significant period. They weren't just to be *doing time,* but they were to have an effect in the society that they found themselves in.

If we are going to reform society and turn it into a demonstration of the kingdom of God on earth, we must lose a temporal mindset, plant our feet, and not be waiting to go to heaven. We are never told to focus on leaving earth and its societies, but rather to take the kingdom of God and change the earth into the splendid glory of Jesus Himself. His awesomeness and glory of who He is demands this to happen.

Jeremiah prophetically told the Jews who found themselves in this heathen place called Babylon that they were to build houses and plant gardens. In other words, they were to inhabit and possess the area and region they were in. If we are going to reform a society, we need to not only build homes but businesses and enterprises as well. We are to be entering the culture of society and establishing businesses that grow into corporations. This is one of the ways we can influence society and its fabric. We are to do business in the society we are in and allow our influence to flow and grow.

They were also to marry wives and beget sons and daughters. Through the expansion of their population, they would take possession of society and of culture and alter it toward a kingdom perspective. The truth is that birthing and raising children who have a kingdom perspective is essential to altering society for the long term. Many other groups with different ideas and values other than the Judeo-Christian bent understand this. Muslims are seeking to take over the world not only by making converts to Islam, but primarily by having multiple children and large families who will eventually outnumber anything that is Christian and carry their mandate into the nations. They understand what most of the Christian world has forgotten. We are to be fruitful and multiply and replenish the earth (see Genesis 1:28). It isn't that we need more human beings on the planet—it is that we need the right kind of human beings on the planet who share the agenda of God, which is His rule of the earth. Being fruitful and multiplying empowers us to subdue the earth under the kingdom rule of God and see society altered and changed. The aforementioned scripture in Genesis 1:28 says:

> *Then God blessed them, and God said to them, "Be fruitful and multiply; fill the earth and subdue it; have dominion over the fish of the sea, over the birds of the air, and over every living thing that moves on the earth."*

Fruitfulness and multiplication that brings dominion can involve the literal birthing of children into families where they grow up having been impregnated with God's divine purpose for their life. How we need to see this occur! We will talk more about this when we get to the family mountain. But multiplication and fruitfulness can also imply and involve the conversion of people to be radical followers of Jesus. If we can see enough people truly born again with the kingdom message pulsating in their bosom, we can penetrate society and its mountain as well. We must realize that this will require something different than what we've seen in the American church up until now. We are not talking about the making of converts. We are talking about making disciples who are radically in love with Jesus and have a passion, vision, call, and commissioning from the Lord to change the earth and establish His glorious rule among the nations. If we can see sons and daughters born into the kingdom, carrying apostolic DNA that is earth shaking and nation shaping, we can see the mountains reformed and society begin to reflect His splendor. As I have declared before, *converts make heaven, but disciples make history!*

Jeremiah also told the Jews who found themselves in the strange land of Babylon to "seek the peace of the city, for in its peace you will have peace." They were also to pray for the city in which they found themselves. Seeking the peace of the city involves the methodical and even slow introduction of the principles of the kingdom of God into everyday life of government, business, education, and the other mountains. The Lord was emphatic—as the city began to experience the peace of the Lord, *only then* would they be able to live in peace as well. We have left these principles behind and not pursued them but have been happy and content if our own personal lives have been blessed. As a result, our children and the coming generations will live in a world that is post-Christian in nature unless there is a radical reformation. We must engage ourselves in prayer and other activities if we are to have any hope of society being altered. We must make cities, regions, nations, and continents our aim if the kingdom of God is going to affect and change society as a whole.

Some alarming statistics are being echoed around our nation right now. We are told that 64 percent of my grandfather's generation were truly born-again believers. My father's generation had 35 percent who were really born again and belonged to the Lord in their spirits. My generation is now down to 16 percent who really love God and serve Him from a true born-again experience. We are being told that unless something happens, my children's generation will be at only 4 percent of those who really know the Lord and serve Him. If these statistics are true—and I believe they are—we are in trouble. We must have a reformation and not just revival hit our society and nation. We truly need, as my friend Dutch Sheets says, an "awakening in our day and reformation in our lifetime." This will require the reformation of each of the seven mountains into the reflection of God's kingdom life so that society as a whole begins to express the Lord's desire in the earth.

Let's take a prophetic look and see what each mountain looks like in a reformed state so we can know what we are shooting for. We will begin with the religion mountain, the family mountain, and the education mountain. I am beginning with these over the next three chapters because these mountains are where the reformers will primarily come from and invade all of the mountains. The religion, family, and education mountains create a triple effect pipeline that will produce reformers to enter the other mountains. As these mountains work together in synergy, reformers with a drive for reformation and a sense of destiny will arise from the religion mountain, the right value system will impregnate from the family mountain, and the right equipping from the education mountain will allow people to enter their individual spheres to see their mountain taken for the kingdom of God. Before we get to this, however, we must see how the Courts of Heaven play into this scenario of revival and reformation. The reclaiming of these mountains and the transforming of society and cultures can only occur when what is controlling them in the unseen world is de-empowered. This requires moving into the Courts of Heaven on a high level. Then and only then can we see these mountains that shape and form society reformed themselves.

CHAPTER 2

CHRISTIAN VS. KINGDOM

I f we are to see the mountains of cultures reformed and society reordered and reclaimed, we must have the right target. I felt the Lord said to me years ago, *"It is possible to hit the target and miss the mark because we are shooting at the wrong thing."* We must be certain of the target we are shooting for. When it comes to the purposes of God in the earth, it seems there are two emphases. One is that the Lord desires *all* to be saved. Second Peter 3:9 is clear with this idea.

> *The Lord is not slack concerning His promise, as some count slackness, but is longsuffering toward us, not willing that any should perish but that all should come to repentance.*

It is the passion of the Lord that all be saved. As I heard my friend Dutch Sheets declare, the *Great Commission* that Jesus gave, which is recorded in Matthew 28 and Mark 16, has these two emphases. One is a personal invitation to be saved and born again. The other is a mandate to see nations discipled and a kingdom culture developed in each. We must understand these two different intents of the Lord. Mark 16:15-18 shows us the personal mandate that Jesus gave His disciples.

> *And He said to them, "Go into all the world and preach the gospel to every creature. He who believes and is baptized will be saved; but he who does not believe will be condemned. And these signs will follow those who believe: In My name they will cast out demons; they will speak with new tongues; they will take up serpents; and if they drink anything deadly, it will by no means hurt them; they will lay hands on the sick, and they will recover."*

This is a Jesus telling His disciples that they are to preach the gospel to mankind. They are to endeavor to get every single individual saved, healed, delivered, and freed. This is one of the two main agendas of God. The other desire of the Lord is the reformation of culture. Matthew 28:18-19 records Jesus telling us to disciple *nations.*

> *And Jesus came and spoke to them, saying, "All authority has been given to Me in heaven and on*

earth. Go therefore and make disciples of all the nations, baptizing them in the name of the Father and of the Son and of the Holy Spirit."

The *making disciples of all nations* means that not only are massive numbers of individuals to be saved, but the society and cultures of nations are to be transformed as well. This is where we must understand the difference between something being *Christian or kingdom*. Obviously, it is our desire and Jesus' passion that every person on the earth would be born again. This is what it means to be a *Christian*. However, this is impractical when it comes to culture and society as a whole. If we try and make a nation *Christian*, then we can inadvertently be seeking to create a religious state. In other words, we are desiring and shooting at a target that we don't really need or want. We could end up with a Christian version of the Taliban that rules in Afghanistan or other places. This is why the founding fathers of America sought to avert this. They wanted *religious freedom*, not a *religious state*.

With this said, we do want a *kingdom culture* in our nations. This means that although we are not a Christian version of a religious state, we are a nation with a kingdom *culture*. When Jesus said to make *disciples of all nations*, He was beckoning us to change the thinking of a nation until it reflects the core ideas of the kingdom of God. Its culture becomes an expression of the kingdom of God in the earth. This can happen without everyone being Christian. So to be clear, we want all to be saved and be Christian. However, we want our nations to be kingdom in their thinking and culture. This is what it means to disciple nations.

So what is a *kingdom culture?* It is the *morals, ethics, values, and virtues* of the King made manifest. A kingdom culture in a nation is when Jesus' nature is made manifest in that society. The culture/society begins to function with the morals, ethics, values, and virtues that are a part of who Jesus is. It is possible for this to operate without everyone being a Christian. This is because a culture of the kingdom of God has taken hold of a society.

In my lifetime, I have seen some semblance of this in America. There was a time in America when there was a premium placed on godly values, morals, ethics, and virtues. They were applauded and expected within our culture. This began to slip away in the 1960s. These ideas, which were actually kingdom of God concepts, began to be eroded and eventually washed away. The church did little or nothing to stop this devilish process. One of the main culprits that allowed this was a bad eschatology. In other words, an idea that the devil was going to take over nations; therefore, all this had to happen so Jesus could come back. This idea is still present in a large part of the church today.

My purpose in this book is not to get into end-time ideas; however, what one believes is important. It will either motivate you to take up a kingdom agenda or cause you to allow the devil and his forces to rule nations. Many times, I tell people that I don't care what their eschatology is as long as it leaves room for reformation of culture. However, the truth is that we should have an end-time view that coincides with God's heart for discipling nations! I would suggest Harold Eberle's book *Victorious Eschatology* as a text to help understand these things.

Our call and commission from the Lord is to see as many people born again, saved, healed, and delivered as possible. It is also to change nations into a kingdom way of thinking that coincides with Jesus' nature as King. This is what it means to *disciple.* When we disciple something, we are altering the thinking of that person or thing. This is what we must do within nations. It is the seven mountains of culture that create the thinking of a nation and society. Therefore, to change the way a nation thinks or to disciple it, these mountains must be reformed. They presently are shaping the thinking of the culture in a wrong way. However, as we understand our goal/target we are shooting at, we can see these mountains changed. The result will be a nation developing a kingdom heart.

In recent times there have been charges of *nationalism* leveled at the church. Those of us who believe we are not only here to see individuals saved but nations discipled have been charged with this accusation. Nationalism defined means "an ideology that *emphasizes loyalty, devotion, or allegiance to a nation or nation-state* and holds that such obligations outweigh other individual or group interests."

In our day, this has become an ugly word. To justify this attack against people who have a heart for their geographical nation, there has been an altering of concepts in portions of the church. The issue that has arisen is the definition of *nations.* Remember that Jesus charged us with making disciples of all nations. The word *nation* in the Greek is *ethnos.* It means by definition to be "a race, a tribe, a nation." Those who are now espousing contradicting ideas are saying that the commission of Jesus was not to change geographical nations but simply the culture of people groups. The dangerous result of this philosophy is giving over into the devil's hands geographical and political nations that are ruling the earth.

I will address later where some of these ideas are stemming from. Suffice it to say here that America is a nation made up of *nations*. There are many different races, people groups, etc. in the nation of America. It is my opinion that if we do our job and make disciples of nations/*ethnos*, we will in fact see the discipling of political nations as well. Without this reality, we will lose nations to the antichrist agenda. Instead of us being a part of seeing every enemy brought under His footstool, we will be repeating the gross error of abdicating our God-ordained authority once again.

As we have seen throughout history, our lack of involvement in these matters will allow the satanic forces to take over our cultures. You only have to look at the last 50 years in America to see the fruit of this view. The legality of abortion, the disintegration of the family, prayer removed from school, an educational system progressively and radically anti-God, and many other things have occurred. All this happened because the church withdrew from being the salt of the earth and the light of the world within culture. This attack of *nationalism* against the church is nothing more than an intimidation tactic to remove us once again from exercising our influence in political matters. This will not end well for our culture and God's agenda in it, should this be allowed.

With this said, I watched in great frustration and even horror as the attack ensued against the presidency of Donald Trump. I am not talking about the attack from the liberal anti-God media. I am talking about the attack from Christian circles. Obviously, Donald Trump is far from perfect. Many of his decisions can easily be seen as egotistical and self-centered. However, it is my opinion that he is in fact a Cyrus who was raised up for just this time in history. Cyrus was a heathen king who was mightily used by God to rebuild and reinstitute the nation of Israel after its captivity. God placed it in his heart to send the nation of Israel back to its land with wealth and all that was needed to rebuild. Even though he was a wicked and evil king by *Christian* standards, God still called him His anointed one and His shepherd. Isaiah 44:28 and Isaiah 45:1 both speak to this.

> *Who says of Cyrus, "He is My shepherd,*
> *And he shall perform all My pleasure,*
> *Saying to Jerusalem, 'You shall be built,'*
> *And to the temple, 'Your foundation shall be*
> *laid.'"*

> *...Thus says the Lord to His anointed,*
> *To Cyrus, whose right hand I have held –*
> *To subdue nations before him*
> *And loose the armor of kings,*
> *To open before him the double doors,*
> *So that the gates will not be shut.*

In both of these verses, the Lord proclaims that Cyrus is His instrument and vessel. The Lord is declaring this not as an approval of his morals but of his heart to move in agreement with the will of God in the earth. The truth is that Cyrus was used by God in spite of his wickedness to fulfill God's *kingdom will.*

This is exactly what God did with and through President Donald J. Trump. People debate whether Donald Trump is a Christian or not. The truth is it doesn't matter! God did not set Donald Trump in as president as a result of him being a Christian. He set him in because of His kingdom heart. The sad fact is that a great portion of the church cannot see this. Therefore, they spoke against him and were party to removing him from office. All because of a religious spirit taking advantage of a Christian perspective rather than a kingdom one! Those who criticized President Trump for a less-than-Christian performance while in office were themselves beset by a religious, fault-finding spirit. This was because they were more interested in having a Christian president rather than a kingdom one. We are suffering and will suffer the consequences of this. When we reject a reformer sent by God, which I believe President Trump to be, we will come under the disciplining hand of God. This is what is happening in America and will continue to happen until things have run their course.

I am stating these things to seek to bring us to an awareness that when we talk about the reformation of the mountains and therefore our society and culture, we must think kingdom and not Christian. We desire everyone to be born again and be a Christian so they can have eternal life. However, when we speak of the redeeming of society, we must think kingdom. As we will see throughout the remainder of this book, this is what our goal should be. We must be shooting at the right target so we don't miss the mark. May God grant us grace to understand.

CHAPTER 3

REVOKING LEGAL CLAIMS FROM THE COURTS OF HEAVEN

From the outset of the revelation of the Courts of Heaven, I knew it had social and cultural significance. I intuitively understood that the intent of God for the nations was locked up in this principle. Even in the days of Daniel, when he as a prophetic person *watched and saw* the Courts in operation, it was on a social, cultural, and even global level. Daniel 7:9-10 unveils the judicial system of heaven. We see it operating in its glory and splendor.

> *I watched till thrones were put in place,*
> *And the Ancient of Days was seated;*
> *His garment was white as snow,*
> *And the hair of His head was like pure wool.*
> *His throne was a fiery flame,*
> *Its wheels a burning fire;*

> *A fiery stream issued*
> *And came forth from before Him.*
> *A thousand thousands ministered to Him;*
> *Ten thousand times ten thousand stood before*
> *Him.*
> *The court was seated,*
> *And the books were opened.*

Daniel beheld the Lord as the Ancient of Days ruling over the Courts of Heaven. He is the One who renders decisions from this Court that alter life on planet Earth. When this Court sets a decision in place, there is no appealing it. In later verses of Daniel 7, we see the power of this Court. In verses 25-27 we see the antichrist being judged.

> *He shall speak pompous words against the Most*
> *High,*
> *Shall persecute the saints of the Most High,*
> *And shall intend to change times and law.*
> *Then the saints shall be given into his hand*
> *For a time and times and half a time.*
>
> *But the court shall be seated,*
> *And they shall take away his dominion,*
> *To consume and destroy it forever.*
> *Then the kingdom and dominion,*
> *And the greatness of the kingdoms under the*
> *whole heaven,*

*Shall be given to the people, the saints of the
Most High.
His kingdom is an everlasting kingdom,
And all dominions shall serve and obey Him.*

The arrogant and rebellious antichrist is judged and destroyed by courtroom activity. In other words, the nations and cultures are freed from this spirit of antichrist that has fashioned the thinking of nations. Notice that one verdict from this Court moves the saints from defeat to dominion. They had been under the hand of this diabolical spirit but now were given dominion over the kingdoms of earth. This all occurred because of a single verdict/decision from this Court.

If we are to see societies, cultures, and nations claimed for the kingdom of God, we must know how to function in the Courts of Heaven. The Courts of Heaven is not a place of the sovereign activity of God. It is the place where cases are made by the people of God that allow divine judgments to come. This causes nations and their societies and cultures to be freed from demonic rule. This is clear from the judgment of this antichrist spirit in the occasion we have read about.

One of the reasons we know we have influence in the Courts is because Jesus actually put prayer in a judicial setting. In the book of Luke, while teaching on prayer, Jesus placed prayer in three dimensions. He set prayer as approaching God as *Father,* as *Friend,* and as *Judge.* Let me show you these three ideas.

When the disciples asked Jesus about prayer, He responded by telling them initially that God should be approached as their Father. Luke 11:1-2 gives us this understanding.

> *Now it came to pass, as He was praying in a certain place, when He ceased, that one of His disciples said to Him, "Lord, teach us to pray, as John also taught his disciples."*
>
> *So He said to them, "When you pray, say:*
> *Our Father in heaven,*
> *Hallowed be Your name.*
> *Your kingdom come.*
> *Your will be done*
> *On earth as it is in heaven."*

All prayer and all the development of a prayer life must begin out of a revelation of God as Father. When we know by revelation that the Lord is our Father, this grants us the right basis on which to approach Him. This revelation comes through the person of the Holy Spirit. Romans 8:15 calls the Holy Spirit the *Spirit of adoption.*

> *For you did not receive the spirit of bondage again to fear, but you received the Spirit of adoption by whom we cry out, "Abba, Father."*

Notice that the Holy Spirit as the Spirit of adoption unveils God as our intimate Father who loves us. This creates a cry or prayer in our hearts toward Him. All prayer should originate from this place of understanding granted by revelation.

The second means of approaching God was revealed as Jesus continued to speak. In Luke 11:5-8, Jesus talked of coming to God as our *Friend.*

> *And He said to them, "Which of you shall have a friend, and go to him at midnight and say to him, 'Friend, lend me three loaves; for a friend of mine has come to me on his journey, and I have nothing to set before him'; and he will answer from within and say, 'Do not trouble me; the door is now shut, and my children are with me in bed; I cannot rise and give to you'? I say to you, though he will not rise and give to him because he is his friend, yet because of his persistence he will rise and give him as many as he needs."*

As Jesus continued to teach His disciples about prayer in response to their question, He talked of a person who had a friend who came to him on his journey. He had nothing to help him get to his destination or destiny. He therefore arose and went to another friend who had provision. He got him out of bed and he received as much as he needed. This is the picture of approaching the Lord as our Friend on behalf of someone else. When we approach God as Father, it is primarily for our own need. However, when we approach Him as Friend it is on behalf of someone else. We can pray on behalf of others and see God provide what they need for their journey to their destiny. This was the second dimension of prayer.

The third realm is found in Luke 18:1-8. Jesus placed prayer in a judicial system in this story/parable. He spoke of a widow coming before an unjust judge. An adversary had a legal case against her. Through her persistent presentation of her case, the judge gave her a right verdict.

> *Then He spoke a parable to them, that men always ought to pray and not lose heart, saying: "There was in a certain city a judge who did not fear God nor regard man. Now there was a widow in that city; and she came to him, saying, 'Get justice for me from my adversary.' And he would not for a while; but afterward he said within himself, 'Though I do not fear God nor regard man, yet because this widow troubles me I will avenge her, lest by her continual coming she weary me.'"*
>
> *Then the Lord said, "Hear what the unjust judge said. And shall God not avenge His own elect who cry out day and night to Him, though He*

bears long with them? I tell you that He will
avenge them speedily. Nevertheless, when the
Son of Man comes, will He really find faith on
the earth?"

The whole moral to the story is that if this widow, without any influence or power, could convince a judge to render a verdict in her favor, how much more can we come before God the righteous Judge and see Him favor us in His decisions. There are several things we should see in this process of approaching God as Judge. First of all, God is the Judge and rules over the judicial system of heaven. Hebrews 12:23 tells us that God is the Judge of *all*. He is taking into account that which is being presently done in the earth.

To the general assembly and church of the first-
born who are registered in heaven, to God the
Judge of all, to the spirits of just men made
perfect.

Presently, God reveals Himself as the Judge to whom we have come. This is a revelation of who He is right now for us. Peter in I Peter 1:17 tells is that God as our Father is judging without partiality.

And if you call on the Father, who without
partiality judges according to each one's work,

conduct yourselves throughout the time of your
stay here in fear.

As a result of this, we are to walk in the fear of the Lord in this life. Our works will be judged by God. Also, as God He can and will render decisions for us from His Courts that He oversees as Judge. Isaiah 43:26 clearly lets us know that we can come and present cases in this Court just like the widow did.

Put Me in remembrance;
Let us contend together;
State your case, that you may be acquitted.

Putting God in remembrance as a means of presenting cases in His Courts is essential. A Judge can only render decisions based on evidence presented. He may know the evidence, but unless an attorney presents it, he is forbidden from considering it in a case. We must know how to present cases in the Courts of Heaven. If we don't, then what God desires to happen cannot and will not occur. There must be a case presented, just like the widow did. I want to point out several things from this story that will encourage and help us in presenting cases in the Courts of Heaven for the reformation of culture and the reclaiming of the mountains of influence.

First of all, this woman has an *adversary*. Luke 18:3 shows her asking for judgment and justice from her *adversary*.

> *Now there was a widow in that city; and she came to him, saying, "Get justice for me from my adversary."*

The Greek word for *adversary* is *antidikos*. This word means "an opponent in a lawsuit." We have a legal opponent that is resisting the will of God. First Peter 5:8 clearly lets us know that this *adversary* is looking for legal means to devour and destroy.

> *Be sober, be vigilant; because your adversary the devil walks about like a roaring lion, seeking whom he may devour.*

This word *adversary* is the same word in the Greek that we found in Luke 18:3. It implies and declares we have a *legal opponent*. We are to be on guard against this legal agent, who is the devil! Otherwise, he will claim the legal right to devour and destroy the will, desire, and intent of God on all levels. This includes the social level and the mountains of culture. He makes cases against us and our societies based on their sin presently and in their history. This is why we see Jesus' manner of warfare against the power of darkness. Revelation 19:11 gives great insight into how Jesus Himself deals with the powers seeking to dominate and influence cultures.

> *Now I saw heaven opened, and behold, a white horse. And He who sat on him was called Faithful and True, and in righteousness He judges and makes war.*

Notice that Jesus has an order in which He does warfare. He *judges* then *makes war. Judging* is judicial activity, while *making war* is battlefield. We have been taught in an insufficient way that we should *bind* and *loose* the devil with no thought for the legal aspect behind these ideas. This has resulted in ineffectiveness and backlash against those who have employed it. Anytime we challenge powers of darkness that yet claim legal rights based on the sin of a culture, they will withstand us and attack us. However, if we go into the Courts of Heaven, take the work of Jesus, and annul these claims, they can be easily removed from influence and power. Zechariah 3:9 tells us that *iniquity can be removed in a day.* This means that what the devil is claiming as his legal right can be revoked when there are those who represent the culture standing in the Courts of Heaven.

> *"For behold, the stone*
> *That I have laid before Joshua:*

Upon the stone are seven eyes.
Behold, I will engrave its inscription,"
Says the Lord of hosts,
"And I will remove the iniquity of that land in
one day."

If you should read the entire account in Zechariah 3, you would find that once Joshua the high priest was restored in his ability to represent the culture before the Lord, the legal claims of the devil to resist restoration were rebuked. Iniquity that was being used by these powers of darkness to legally operate was taken away in *one day*. This means that without decades of prayer, intercession, and repenting, when the *right* ones stood before the Lord to represent society in the Courts, every legal thing was set into place. The claims of the devil were revoked and blessings began to flow back over the nation. Zechariah 3:10 declares, in connection to iniquity being removed in a day, that a spirit of reconciliation began to flow through the culture.

"In that day," says the Lord of hosts,
"Everyone will invite his neighbor
Under his vine and under his fig tree."

The *iniquity being removed in a day* caused all the powers of darkness to lose their rights to divide. A unity was created and set into place. Everyone invited his neighbor under his vine and fig tree. One of the major problems facing cultures today is the division and hostility in our societies. There is presently great anger and outrage among people. Everything is politically parted, socially separated, and racially riven. If there were a group who knew how to represent their culture before the Lord, the iniquity the devil is using to bring this destruction could be stripped from him. There would be a healing of our cultures and society because the legal claims of the devil in the Courts of Heaven have been taken away. How we need those who can represent cultures and the seven mountains that fashion them to stand in these Courts.

In the next chapter, we will see who this group is that has the right to bring a case on behalf of culture and the shapers of said culture, the seven mountains. We must have that which heaven recognizes to stand on behalf of these mountains. Otherwise, we will be less than effective. We will continue to *beat the air* with no measurable results. This is not our lot to be lived. God has ordained that we see results and watch as society is reclaimed for the purposes of God. Stay tuned! We will discover *who* can stand before the Lord and see His passion fulfilled and our nations reclaimed.

CHAPTER 4

A HOUSE OF PRAYER

J ust like a natural court requires those who practice law to be recognized, so it is in the heavenly courts or the Courts of Heaven. There must be a people who are recognized to be able to present cases in the Courts of Heaven on behalf of the mountains of society and culture. Each one of us as individuals can represent ourselves and our families in these Courts. We are told in Hebrews 10:19 that we can enter the holiest place by the Blood of Jesus.

> *Therefore, brethren, having boldness to enter the Holiest by the blood of Jesus.*

The *Holiest* is a reference to what is called the *Holiest of Holies* in other places. This is the place that only the high priest could enter once a year to make atonement for himself and the people. It was the place where the blood of the Passover lamb was sprinkled and poured out to *legally* secure forgiveness and redemption. We are told that we now have access into this place. In this *legal place* in the spirit, we can operate in the Courts of Heaven. We can by faith appropriate the Blood of our Passover Lamb. His name is Jesus. In this Holiest of Holies, we call into remembrance the activity of Jesus on behalf of us and our families. The Blood of sprinkling in this place speaks for us according to Hebrews 12:24.

> *To Jesus the Mediator of the new covenant, and to the blood of sprinkling that speaks better things than that of Abel.*

Abel's blood cried for judgment; however, the Blood of Jesus cries for redemption and forgiveness. Jesus' Blood silences every voice against us that would dare to speak. When we know how to present this as evidence in the Courts of Heaven, we get the full benefit of all Jesus has done for us and our families. This is the privilege we have as individuals. However, when it comes to society, cultures, and the mountains that shape culture, biblically only a *House of Prayer* has the right to represent these. Without a House of Prayer standing on behalf of a culture, claims against a culture cannot be dismissed. We find this in Isaiah 56:7.

> *Even them I will bring to My holy mountain,*
> *And make them joyful in My house of prayer.*

> *Their burnt offerings and their sacrifices*
> *Will be accepted on My altar;*
> *For My house shall be called a house of prayer*
> *for all nations.*

The Lord promises to take certain ones and build His House of Prayer. Notice that this *House* will stand on behalf of nations. Every culture and society must have a House of Prayer representing it before the Lord. This is what has the right and privilege to present cases for society and the mountains that fashion it. A House of Prayer that has been formed and built can stand in God's *Holy Mountain* and present prayers and petitions for the nation it is a part of.

The phrase *My Holy Mountain* is not speaking of a geographical high place. It is speaking of a governmental place in the spirit realm. As this House of Prayer stands in these governmental places, they can present petitions to the Lord that will grant Him the legal right to redeem cultures and societies. We see the absence of this in the days of Sodom and Gomorrah. The Lord agreed with Abraham that if there were ten righteous, He would spare this wicked place. Genesis 18:32 shows the Lord willing to spare this place if there were ten righteous.

> *Then he said, "Let not the Lord be angry, and I*
> *will speak but once more: Suppose ten should be*

*found there?" And He said, "I will not destroy it
for the sake of ten."*

Think about this idea. God was willing to not bring destruction to this evil people and place if there were ten righteous ones there. In other words, if there were ten righteous who could represent the cause of this place, the Lord as Judge would allow the city and region to continue. We are told that there were up to 65,000 who lived in this place. The Lord is willing to allow the influence of 10 righteous to stand on behalf of 65,000. These 10 righteous could secure mercy and grace for 65,000. When these 10 righteous would repent for the 65,000, the Lord would esteem it as if the whole 65,000 had repented. This is because the 10 righteous would constitute a House of Prayer on behalf of this culture. This would have been a practical playing out and demonstration of God's House being a House of Prayer for all nations. The problem was, there were not 10 righteous. Therefore, the city and region were judged and destroyed. If we are to see the mountains of society and cultures reclaimed, there must be houses of prayer to represent them. Only when a House is built that can stand and represent them will God be granted the legal right to redeem.

One of our big problems is we think that if a bunch of disjointed people say prayers for the nation/

mountains/cultures/societies, God will hear and respond. However, the word of the Lord is clear. Only a house can secure mercy for cultures and its influencers. This is why the spirit of competition must be repented of and removed from our midst. Until our passion for His will to be done in the earth supersedes our desire for credit and glory, we will not see a House of Prayer arise that can do what is being described. There can and should be many different expressions of a House of Prayer. However, when there is something on a national level that is threatening the destiny and future of that nation, we must be willing to come together without thought of vain glory. We must be willing to lay aside all such things and take up the cause that is before us. We can see this in Zechariah 12:10-14.

> *And I will pour on the house of David and on the inhabitants of Jerusalem the Spirit of grace and supplication; then they will look on Me whom they pierced. Yes, they will mourn for Him as one mourns for his only son, and grieve for Him as one grieves for a firstborn. In that day there shall be a great mourning in Jerusalem, like the mourning at Hadad Rimmon in the plain of Megiddo. And the land shall mourn, every family by itself: the family of the house of David by itself, and their wives by themselves; the family*

> *of the house of Nathan by itself, and their wives*
> *by themselves; the family of the house of Levi by*
> *itself, and their wives by themselves; the family*
> *of Shimei by itself, and their wives by themselves;*
> *all the families that remain, every family by itself,*
> *and their wives by themselves.*

The Lord promises to pour out an anointing of grace and supplication that will empower us to pray. This power to pray will cause us to pray into reality all that Jesus died for. This is actually the whole purpose of prayer. As we get a revelation of what Jesus died for us to have through the New Covenant, we then pray it into place under the spirit of grace and supplication. Notice, however, that this intercession that is birthed through this anointing will cause *whole families* to mourn. This is the prophet describing the intercession of houses of prayer. This means there are multiple houses of prayer contending in the spirit under the assignment given them. However, there is a time for these *families* to come together for the purpose of the whole culture. The result will be a fountain being opened that sets things in order, even on national and cultural levels. We see this in the next verses of Zechariah 13:1-5. These verses describe the results of these *families/houses* of prayer functioning together.

"In that day a fountain shall be opened for the house of David and for the inhabitants of Jerusalem, for sin and for uncleanness.

"It shall be in that day," says the Lord of hosts, "that I will cut off the names of the idols from the land, and they shall no longer be remembered. I will also cause the prophets and the unclean spirit to depart from the land. It shall come to pass that if anyone still prophesies, then his father and mother who begot him will say to him, 'You shall not live, because you have spoken lies in the name of the Lord.' And his father and mother who begot him shall thrust him through when he prophesies.

"And it shall be in that day that every prophet will be ashamed of his vision when he prophesies; they will not wear a robe of coarse hair to deceive. But he will say, 'I am no prophet, I am a farmer; for a man taught me to keep cattle from my youth.'"

Notice that a fountain or a move of God is opened from the prayer of these houses of prayer. The result of this is five-fold. This fountain that opens because of houses of prayer functioning causes people to know God is for them. We are told the fountain is *for* the inhabitants of Jerusalem and the House of David.

This means that a culture/society is being impacted by what houses of prayer have opened up. The second thing we are told is it is for sins and uncleanness. This means that the shame and guilt of secret sins is destroyed. When this fountain opens, people are freed from that which has secretly dominated them. We are then told that there will be pure worship reinstated. No longer will people speak of the names of idols. The name of the Lord will be exalted and extolled instead. The prophetic will also be purified as a result of the houses of prayer that open this fountain.

Finally, people will discover and acknowledge their true calling. They will no longer try to operate in a mountain not ordained for them. They will become settled in what they actually were created for and the grace they carry. This is seen when those who are trying to be prophets or are operating in the *religion mountain* realize and admit they are actually business people in the business mountain. This is what it means to be a farmer. When the houses of prayer began to function under the spirit of grace and supplication, this fountain will be open that will bring revival, order, and reformation to culture.

These houses of prayer are absolutely essential to the mountains of culture being reclaimed. Without them, we can never grant the Lord the legal right to fulfill His passion. Each culture must have houses of prayer to represent this culture. In contending for Sodom and Gomorrah, Abraham himself didn't ask God to spare it. This was always curious to me, until I saw that Abraham was not from Sodom and Gomorrah. Therefore, he had no right to represent it to the Lord. It seems that a House of Prayer that can successfully stand in the Courts of Heaven must be a part of the culture it is representing. Ezekiel 22:30-31 bears this out.

> *"So I sought for a man among them who would make a wall, and stand in the gap before Me on behalf of the land, that I should not destroy it; but I found no one. Therefore I have poured out My indignation on them; I have consumed them with the fire of My wrath; and I have recompensed their deeds on their own heads,"* says the Lord God.

Notice that God sought for a man *among them*. This means that whoever had the right to stand for the culture/society/mountains had to be *from* them. Abraham wasn't from Sodom and Gomorrah. Therefore, he had no legal basis to represent them in the Court of Heaven. His role was to seek to *pray* into place a House of Prayer that could represent them. He wasn't able to get this done; therefore, the area was judged and destroyed. We must have houses of prayer to stand and contend for our cultures/societies and mountains. As these are formed under the spirit of grace and supplication, there will be the right granted the Lord to redeem our nations as mountains of culture are reclaimed.

Each mountain should have a House of Prayer from within these mountains. These people have an unusual authority to shift things and revoke the claims of demonic powers controlling these mountains. As the Spirit of the Lord forms these houses of prayer even within individual mountains, they will have the ability to present cases on behalf of these society shapers. If someone is called to a specific mountain, it would seem that a part of that call is to bind together with others with similar calls to pray. This can result in presenting cases in the courts to diffuse powers of darkness and see their dominion over the mountains revoked.

A great help to this process is to understand this is what the Courts of Heaven are for. In Luke 18:6-8, Jesus gives us the lesson He is communicating. As He speaks of the widow that keeps presenting her case, He declares this is what we as the elect of God should do.

> *Then the Lord said, "Hear what the unjust judge said. And shall God not avenge His own elect who cry out day and night to Him, though He bears long with them? I tell you that He will avenge them speedily. Nevertheless, when the*

Son of Man comes, will He really find faith on the earth?"

This widow was an outsider in the Court of this unjust judge. Jesus was declaring that if she could get a decision rendered, how much more we as the *elect of God*. This means the Court of Heaven is the place where the *elect* bring cases against the powers of darkness. Remember that the *adversary* is the *antidikos* or one who is attacking us with a lawsuit. However, we as the elect of God have the right to counter-sue and bring a case against him. This is the *best way* to do spiritual warfare. We come with our repentance, Jesus' work on our behalf, and all the other spiritual activity operating for us and present our case. As a result the Judge of All renders a verdict for us as the elect of God. You do not need to be afraid, bashful, or timid in coming before His Courts. We have been chosen in Him before time began according to Ephesians 1:4.

Just as He chose us in Him before the foundation of the world, that we should be holy and without blame before Him in love.

We are holy and without blame in Him. We are chosen by Him. Therefore, we have a special place in the Courts of Heaven as the chosen/elect of God to present cases that allow the Lord to judge the powers of darkness. As we stand as a House of Prayer in this chosen place, God hears our petitions. Unlike Sodom and Gomorrah, mercy is shown, mountains of culture are reclaimed, and society is transformed. Don't allow intimidation to keep you from being a part of the House of Prayer and coming boldly as His elect into the Courts of Heaven. We will reshape the cultures we are a part of as judgments are made from heaven. The mountains we are called to will begin to take on the nature and likeness mandated and dictated by God. Our nations and cultures will begin to look more like heaven than like hell. Let's take our place in the Courts of Heaven and see earth manifest His glory!

CHAPTER 5

THE REFORMED RELIGION MOUNTAIN
Part 1: The Impetus Mountain

The religion mountain is much more than the expression of the Christian church. If we limit the religion mountain to just the *church*, we exempt many other expressions of religion. If we do this, we will not be able to see a reformation of this sphere in reality. At best, we will have only a partial representation of reformation. We must understand that we are going after the reformation of the whole of religion within our society and not just the church.

Having said this, the church is the entity that will bring reformation to all the mountains—including the religion mountain. Because the church is presently unable to do this as a result of its belief system, it is in a reformation process itself. As the church is reformed from being a caregiver or pastoral in nature into a people of reformation—who are out to change the world and are apostolic in nature—it will become the driving force for reformation from the religion mountain. The drive or impetus for reformation will come from the religion mountain for all of the mountains. None of the other mountains or molders of culture have the capacity or vision to see society reformed. Only the church within the religion mountain has this ability. Therefore, the religion mountain is the *impetus mountain.*

From this mountain will sound forth the need, desire, and cry for reformation. The church within this mountain will be the epicenter for social reformation. This will require a *voice* to come forth from this mountain. That which drives reformations does so with a voice, at least initially. This is what John the Baptist was. Prophetically speaking, he was a voice of one crying out. We see this in his response when asked who he was in John 1:22-23.

> *Then they said to him, "Who are you, that we may give an answer to those who sent us? What do you say about yourself?"*
>
> *He said: "I am 'The voice of one crying in the wilderness:*
> *"Make straight the way of the Lord,"'*
> *as the prophet Isaiah said."*

John was used by God to start a reformation that Jesus would continue. He came as a voice to drive or be the impetus of this reformation. The nation of Israel had severely corrupted the ways of God. They had painted a picture of the Lord that was skewed and incorrect. John came declaring a true image of who the Lord was and commanded people to repent. This was in preparation for Jesus' coming on the scene.

My point is that every reformation starts with a voice that becomes the impetus of that reformation. This means that the message of the church might need to be rethought. I'm not saying we shouldn't preach Jesus, the cross, His resurrection, and other central points. I am saying that in addition there should be a message that stirs the hearts of people to be reformers. We need this heart stimulated in the church until there is a passion to give ourselves for a cause. This is because people become aware that they as a kingdom/apostolic people are here to see His kingdom come. This will cause a deep sense of destiny to take hold and motivate people to lay their life down for His kingdom rule. From within the church, there must be voices raised who will challenge the present viewpoint. These viewpoints are the result of drifting from the true revelation of the Lord and His ways. This will mandate certain things happening.

In order to be a force of reformation, the church within the religion mountain must begin to view life differently. This understanding changes our perspective and what *religion versus the church* looks like in a reformed state.

When we talk of the mountain of religion, we are speaking of all expressions of religion in our society — not just the Christian church. This includes Islam, New Age, Hinduism, Judaism, and groups considered cults — Jehovah's Witnesses, Mormons, and many others. Some believe that we don't need to reform these groups; instead, we need to get them saved, born again, and out of their deception. I agree that the ultimate intent of the Lord is to see the folks involved in these expressions of religion within our society come to a true awareness and saving experience with Jesus. But in the absence of this, we must take a look at the reality of the matter. There will never be the whole of humanity on earth recognizing Jesus as Lord and Savior until His physical return to earth. Until that time, our mission from the Lord is to reclaim the earth and its societies back under the authority of the King and His kingdom. This does not mean that all people are saved or that they all believe in Jesus the way we do or even at all. It means that religion in our society becomes a source of life into the planet, if only for the span of men's lives here.

In other words, we are not speaking of the eternal state of man when we refer to the mountain of religion, but rather of the effect of this mountain on society in the earth now. Remember that our agenda is to bring reformation to the earth and its societies in the here and now. Once Jesus returns to the earth, the earth and all of its societies will be changed and come under the domain of the King fully and completely. Up until that time, it is our job and mission to see these mountains, including religion, release that which is kingdom in nature into the earth even if people from other religious convictions don't completely realize what is happening. This is why we must make the distinction between religion and church. I have personally heard Dennis Peacocke, a great Christian thinker along these lines, proclaim that only when the church learns to partner with unbelievers can the reformation of society begin to be a reality. This is what I am seeking to communicate. We must break free from our evangelical narrow-mindedness and learn to cooperate with people of differing views to see God's kingdom become visibly present through society's transformation.

If we are going to reform the religion mountain, we need to know why there is such a thing as religion in the earth today. By definition *religion* is "the belief in and worship of a superhuman controlling power, especially a personal God or gods." In some form, most people have a belief system rooted in the awareness of a supreme being. In spite of what atheists would have us to believe, this is true. There are five reasons for this and the fact that religions exist in the world.

First of all, religion is designed to make sense of our own existence. Ecclesiastes 3:11 tells us that God has put eternity in the heart of man:

> *He has made everything beautiful in its time. Also He has put eternity in their hearts, except that no one can find out the work that God does from beginning to end.*

There is an innate awareness in man that we are more than the animals we live around and that we were created for a reason. God created us to live forever and to live with purpose. It was never His intention that we die and cease to exist. When Adam was created and placed in the garden, it was an eternal placing in the earth. In spite of the "fall," we still carry this sense in us as human beings. Religion is an outgrowth of that awareness within man. It is man's attempt to satisfy and make sense of our very existence. The belief that there is a God who is in charge and rules the earth helps us in our search for significance and purpose. Thus, many religions have been created to meet this deepest need and awareness within us as human beings. Many have demonic roots, but they are nonetheless there because of the deep need for significance in man.

Another reason for the religion mountain in the earth today is man's need to worship. Man was created by God to be a worshiper. We will worship something. Romans 1:25 tells us that man even in a fallen and rebellious state will worship something:

> *Who exchanged the truth of God for the lie, and worshiped and served the creature rather than the Creator, who is blessed forever. Amen.*

Even in a reprobate state, there is something in man that must worship. We are the creation that was designed to worship the Creator. As a result of our position caused by the fall, our worship can get misdirected. Couple this with the devil's desire to be like the Most High and have worship for himself, and you have a ready-made scenario for many religions to arise. Remember that satan himself tempted Jesus while in the wilderness with the fact that if He would worship him, then the devil would give the kingdoms of the world to Jesus (see Matthew 4:9-10). Of course, Jesus resisted this and told the devil to leave. But the fact remains that there is a great desire within satan for worship directed toward him. Because of this, many religions have their roots in demonic persuasions out of the devil's desire for and man's need to worship. Religions are in the world because of these two dynamics.

Religions also exist out of man's need for supernatural help. There are limitations on us as human beings. Therefore, we will encounter things we can't explain or change in life. This creates a need within man to have a supernatural entity in our life. This is a source of comfort and help. Most religious expressions have a hope that the god they worship will be a present help in the time of trouble. Every human being will face times of need and distress. A supernatural entity provides hope for resolution to the situation they are facing. Religion is the result of this need.

Religion also carries a moral standard for us as humans. In most religious expressions, moral absolutes are present. The power to perform them is another thing, but the expectations are there nonetheless. When Jehovah claimed Israel from Egypt for Himself, He set down the *Law* they were to obey. Within the *Law* were the moral absolutes, among which were the Ten Commandments. Most if not all religious groups, regardless of their persuasions, would adhere to these statutes and standards. Religions provide society with the standards that make us civilized and functional together as a people. Otherwise, everyone would be doing what is right in their own eyes and chaos would soon occur.

A final thought on the existence of religion in our society today is that it compels man to help man. In most religions, there is a reward for compassion and mercy shown toward others at least in the life to come. Regardless of the convictions of a given religious group, there is an awareness of the needs of people. Compassion toward others characterizes most religious groups. This is why Mother Teresa and her life and ministry among the impoverished of India so touched the whole spectrum of the world. Regardless of religious persuasions, she was applauded and renowned for her sacrifice to those in the greatest of need. This is because at the core of the religion mountain there is a commitment to minister to the needs of humanity. As we will see, this is where we can be joined together regardless of what religious expression we employ.

THE REFORMED RELIGION MOUNTAIN
Part 2: The Impetus Mountain

So the question is, what does the religion mountain look like in a reformed state? Again, we are not talking about the Christian church alone, but the church as a part of the mountain of religion, recognizing that it is a driving force or impetus.

To really grasp the reformation of the religion mountain, we must understand the dictates and voice flowing out of I Timothy 4:10:

> *For to this end we both labor and suffer reproach, because we trust in the living God, who is the Savior of all men, especially of those who believe.*

Paul said that God is the Savior of all men, especially those who believe. So we see the passion of the Lord revealed here. God is concerned not just about those who will be saved and go to heaven, but even about those who live their life out here on earth and will be lost. This is a radical statement for most evangelicals. God is the Savior of all men. So this means that if they are not all going to make heaven, God is still concerned with their state here on the earth. This gives great liberty and latitude to us as Christians to involve ourselves with other groups to *save* all men from the perils of the earth. We don't have to have them join us as believers to be the voice and arms of God reaching out to them. Most of the time, we believers have a hidden agenda rather than just loving people and being the "saving grace" of God reaching into their lives while they are here on earth. People can sense this and are resistant to it. We wonder why they won't listen to us in our appeal for them to be saved and go to heaven.

You must understand that I am what Dr. C. Peter Wagner refers to as a charismatically inclined evangelical with a deep passion for people to be saved, born again, and become eternally secure. I believe this is a part of our mandate in the earth. Getting as many people saved as we can is one of the commissioned purposes of the church. Yet if we aren't careful, we can miss an even bigger picture and become isolated bigots in our thinking and end up ostracizing ourselves from the rest of society and the mountain of religion. We are not only to claim souls for the kingdom; we are to make the whole of society a place that reflects the splendor of the King. We are here to make earth a better place to live for those who will go to heaven and for those who will not. What else could this scripture mean when we are told that God is the Savior of all men, especially those who believe? The ones who believe get salvation in this life and the one to come, but all men are to experience His saving power at the least in this life. When this is understood, we can see this happen through the religion mountain. When we adopt this perspective, we will see people actually come to know the Lord Jesus because they will be won by the sincerity of our agenda. We will be accomplishing the two great desires of the Lord: the saving of people from eternal destruction and the reclaiming of the earth and its societies back to God.

This brings me to the next thought concerning the picture of this mountain reformed. At the core of the reformed religion mountain should be an emphasis on the betterment of society and oppressed people groups. Regardless of religious persuasions, there should be a passion and strategy to change what needs to be changed to minister to the needs of people. James 1:26-27 tells us what undefiled religion is:

If anyone among you thinks he is religious, and does not bridle his tongue but deceives his own heart, this one's religion is useless. Pure and undefiled religion before God and the Father is this: to visit orphans and widows in their trouble, and to keep oneself unspotted from the world.

The care of orphans and widows is the job of religion. I realize this was written from a Christian perspective, but this is still the job of anything that is religious in nature. In the reformed religion mountain, there will be the ability to join together with other groups that do not believe as we do and accomplish a common goal for the betterment of society. This is exactly what happened in the civil rights movement of the 1960s led by Dr. Martin Luther King, Jr. Out of the religion mountain, a movement began that impacted and radically reshaped the whole of society. We still feel the effects of this today. Dr. King was a Baptist preacher whose influence was felt far beyond his own congregation. What started in a local congregation exploded and changed society. People from all sorts of perspectives and persuasions joined the movement until society was shaken and reshaped by the force of people coming together for a common goal and good. This is what can and should happen in a reformed religion mountain that is functioning as the impetus mountain.

This can be quite challenging for conservative evangelical Christians. A sense of betrayal can be felt in our hearts if we work with others who are not of our persuasion and are not born again. We must shake free from this idea. We are not compromising ourselves by involving ourselves with other religious groups for the purpose of social betterment. We are simply recognizing that as big as Jesus' passion is for all to be saved and live eternally with Him, He also has a passion to reclaim the earth and make it a reflection and demonstration of His kingdom coming and His will being done. He wants all men to be saved, especially those who believe.

As the religion mountain takes on a reformed appearance, there will be an atmosphere that allows people of different perspectives to work together. We will lose our narrow-mindedness—not our convictions. When we can begin to see the agenda of God in the earth to make it a display of His splendor, then we can give ourselves to that work knowing we are doing God's will. So often people are afraid of being corrupted with others religious ideas and philosophies. If we truly belong to Jesus and His Spirit dwells in us and the church is really making disciples of its people, we do not have to fear. First John 4:4 tells us that that which dwells in us is greater than what is in the world:

> *You are of God, little children, and have overcome them, because He who is in you is greater than he who is in the world.*

When we see and understand this, we are free to interact spiritually and socially with those of other persuasions. We must not treat them as our enemies. We must be settled and established enough in our own belief that we are confident with them rather than intimidated by them. John G. Lake, the great apostle of healing and power, understood this. While in South Africa, he had a part in what was called a *Congress of Religions*. The purpose was to give each representative of varied religions the opportunity to display the heart of their religious beliefs. There were Confucianists, Buddhists, Brahmans, and Yogis, representatives from all the cults of India, Catholics, and rabbis of the Jewish faith. In the midst of this congress, each representative had as much time as they needed to display the power of his religion and belief system. John G. Lake took part in this with no fear or sense of being out of place. There was no anger or fear of being converted away from their beliefs. They were simply reasonable men, reasonably presenting their case for the heart and core of what they believed. The result was the ability to reason together without fear of retribution and rejection.

This is a demonstration of where we must come to in the religion mountain as it is reformed: the ability to respect and honor each other's beliefs enough to work together without being threatened by the other. Quite honestly, this is a tall order for most evangelicals. This is true primarily because we are not settled enough in our own hearts and minds to relate to others this way. The power of God that flowed through John G. Lake's life and the concrete place of his faith in Jesus Christ made him able to function in this way. So will it do for us as well.

The reformed religion mountain must have liberty and freedom in it for all differing religions. Within the context of America, we must realize we are not seeking to create a *religious state*. This is not the idea. We do not want to be ruled by religious clerics as other nations of the earth are. We do not want a state religion. Freedom of religious expression must be treasured and valued. The framework of our founding fathers must be honored. They ran from religious tyranny, and we must never return to it. In the midst of this, there must be the freedom to practice a true religious belief system as long as it doesn't harm someone else. In the reformed religion mountain, this will always be honored, valued, and esteemed.

When the apostle Paul found himself in Athens, his spirit was stirred by the outrageous worship of many different idols (see Acts 17:16). Paul even said to them that they were very "religious" (see Acts 17:22). As Paul waited for his companions to catch up with him in Athens, he sought to invade the religion mountain of Athens. We have commonly referred to this as Mars Hill. Not only was this the governmental seat of Athens, but it was the religious seat as well. Paul's invasion of this sphere was possible because there was clearly a freedom for ideas to be expressed. Acts 17:21 says:

> *For all the Athenians and the foreigners who were there spent their time in nothing else but either to tell or to hear some new thing.*

In other words, the Athenians had and granted a freedom of expression within their religion mountain. This is a characteristic of the religion mountain in a reformed state.

Paul had the ability within this scenario to attempt to make converts. This is also a sign of the religion mountain in a reformed state. There is no outlawing of the work of evangelism. There is freedom to talk with and seek to convert any and all people to one's belief system. Paul did this within the religion mountain of Athens. Acts 17:34 tells us that Paul's words while on Mars Hill convinced and drew some to become disciples of Jesus Christ:

> *However, some men joined him and believed, among them Dionysius the Areopagite, a woman named Damaris, and others with them.*

This is a sign of a reformed religion mountain: liberty for all groups to declare their doctrines and teaching and allow people to respond accordingly.

For Christians, this should not be a threat. If we really believe that Jesus is the Way, the Truth, and the Life, then He will draw people to the Father. If He is lifted up, He will draw all men to Himself (see John 14:6; John 12:32). We are supposed to have that which the world is seeking after. Within a religion mountain that carries these characteristics, it works to our advantage if we are really being *the church* in the earth today.

As Paul was in Athens waiting for his companions, he began to make an attempt at invading the religion mountain of that region. There are some very clear things that Paul did within this scenario. In a quick overview, let's see what they were.

First of all, Paul cared.

> *Now while Paul waited for them at Athens, his spirit was provoked within him when he saw that the city was given over to idols* (Acts 17:16).

The fact that his heart was stirred with the idolatry of the city meant he cared for the people who were trapped by this deceit, but also his passion was to see the kingdom of God invade this devilish place. The result was he was provoked to take a step to impact the religious culture of that region.

Second, he was reasonable.

> *Therefore he reasoned in the synagogue with the Jews and with the Gentile worshipers, and in the marketplace daily with those who happened to be there* (Acts 17:17).

He reasoned with them. He wasn't weird or strange but was reasonable in his arguments as he sought to impact this mountain. We must have the wisdom to be reasonable in our presentations if we are to invade the mountains of religion. This is what Stephen was in the book of Acts. He spoke with a wisdom that they could not resist (see Acts 6:10). As a result, his message is still being heard today.

Third, he took it to the streets.

> *Therefore he reasoned in the synagogue with the*
> *Jews and with the Gentile worshipers, and in the*
> *marketplace daily with those who happened to be*
> *there* (Acts 17:17).

Paul spoke in both the synagogue and also daily in the marketplace. He spoke with the Jews and the Gentile worshipers. Notice that he simply spoke to those who *happened* to be there. As a result, he began to impact the religious culture of the day.

Fourth, he believed God for right encounters.

> *Then certain Epicurean and Stoic philosophers*
> *encountered him. And some said, "What does*
> *this babbler want to say?" Others said, "He*
> *seems to be a proclaimer of foreign gods," because*
> *he preached to them Jesus and the resurrection.*
> *And they took him and brought him to the Are-*
> *opagus, saying, "May we know what this new*
> *doctrine is of which you speak?"* (Acts 17:18-19)

In Paul's faithfulness to speak with those who "happened" to be there, he came in contact with the leaders of the community both spiritually and naturally. He encountered the philosophers of the society. They took him to the Areopagus, which was where the Athenian supreme tribunal and court of morals was held. It was a seat of government both civil and religious. Paul was thrust into a very potentially influential place by a right encounter. God can grant such things to us as well as we seek to invade the mountain of religion.

Finally, he won those who were in places of influence.

> *However, some men joined him and believed, among them Dionysius the Areopagite, a woman named Damaris, and others with them* (Acts 17:34).

Paul won Dionysius the Areopagite to the Lord. He was one of the members of the court who rendered decisions. It is said traditionally that a small group of the early believers in Athens was left under his leadership when Paul left Athens. Their job was to leaven the religious culture by infiltrating it with the presence of the Lord.

God has a plan for the mountain of religion. As we invade this mountain, we will see it reformed into an expression of the kingdom of God in the earth. From religion, the world can be changed, society bettered, and reformers raised to impact the other six mountains. God has a plan for this mountain and the others as well. The church within the religion mountain is the impetus for reformation. May we as His church learn to function and influence in all of the mountains, even the religion mountain that will produce social transformation.

Before we close this subject of the mountain of religion or the impetus mountain, I want to point out a need if we are going to see this mountain reformed into its proper godly function. We must see God's present heart toward other religions and society as a whole. We should recognize that God is *not* angry today. It is so easy for me to think that God is angry with other religions and people who are not of *the truth*. This means believe what I believe. Quite often, I need an attitude adjustment. Second Corinthians 5:17-20 makes a great statement.

> *Therefore, if anyone is in Christ, he is a new creation; old things have passed away; behold, all things have become new. Now all things are of God, who has reconciled us to Himself through*

> *Jesus Christ, and has given us the ministry of reconciliation, that is, that God was in Christ reconciling the world to Himself, not imputing their trespasses to them, and has committed to us the word of reconciliation.*
>
> *Now then, we are ambassadors for Christ, as though God were pleading through us: we implore you on Christ's behalf, be reconciled to God.*

We are told that God did not impute to the world their sins. He instead reconciled Himself back to the world. This means that God is not angry at those who are against Him. He is pleading with them through us to be reconciled back to Him. This is when people are saved. God poured out His wrath on His Son on the cross. God was in Jesus reconciling the world to Himself. All this means that the Lord is no longer angry with the world. Neither should we be! If we can't get this, we will never be able to see the mountain of religion reformed. We will consider the Lord to be angry with them and therefore so are we. However, if we can see that they are loved by God and He longs for them to accept His offer of reconciliation, our attitude changes. We are now in the proper place to see a reforming of the religion mountain occur. This mountain can then sound forth the sound of reformation as the impetus mountain.

PRAYER POINTS
for the Courts of Heaven

1. Pray for the church to be reformed from a caretaking posture to a world-changing perspective as the driving force for reformation from the religion mountain. This requires a shift from the pastoral model to the apostolic model.

2. Pray for a freedom from subtle prejudices that keep the church from working with others from varying persuasions for reformation.

3. Pray for divine encounters with other religious leaders to bring reformation to the religion mountain.

4. Pray for divine strategy for the church and its leaders to be the driving force for reformation in the religion mountain and all the other mountains as well.

5. Pray for reformers to be developed from the religion mountain with a divine sense of destiny for reformation.

As we come before Your Courts, Lord, we ask for the religion mountain to be reclaimed by You. Would You make it the "impetus mountain" that can drive and be a voice of reformation. Especially, Lord, we ask that the church within this mountain would know Your passion to reclaim culture and society. Make Your church a kingdom culture that desires the morals, ethics, values, and virtues of King Jesus to be manifest within society.

We ask before Your Courts that Your church would become apostolic in its nature and function. Make it that which desires the expansion of Your kingdom culture and rule in all places of society.

We also ask before these Courts that we might be delivered from all subtle prejudice that would make us afraid of other religions. Give us a heart to work together where we can for social reformation. We also ask that we might have revelation that You, Lord, are not angry with the world anymore. Therefore, we no longer have a need to be as well. Change our hearts and perspectives, we pray.

We also ask, Lord, that there might be divine strategies unveiled. We acknowledge before Your Courts that we are not wise enough or smart enough to bring reformation. We are absolutely dependent on Your wisdom.

We ask as well that reformers might be raised up with a deep sense of destiny from the religion mountain. May the divine purpose of God be revealed in people so that they would be willing to give their lives for this cause. In Jesus' Name, amen.

CHAPTER 7

THE REFORMED FAMILY MOUNTAIN
Part 1: The Values Mountain

The family mountain is second of the three mountains from which the bulk of reformers will be produced. The religion, family, and education mountains together will provide a pipeline of reformers who can flood a nation and society and result in the reformation that we must have.

The family mountain in a reformed state is of absolute necessity. This mountain, like no other, has been under a perpetual attack for several generations. There has been an all-out assault against this mountain because the family is the cornerstone of our society. Without the traditional family and its values intact, society will eventually fold up and dissolve from its present status. If the family is disintegrated or even redefined from its conventional and traditional place, then society is altered exponentially. Malachi 4:5-6 shows us that improper or out-of-order family structures will release a curse into the societies of the earth:

> *Behold, I will send you Elijah the prophet*
> *Before the coming of the great and dreadful day*
> *of the Lord.*
> *And he will turn*
> *The hearts of the fathers to the children,*
> *And the hearts of the children to their fathers,*
> *Lest I come and strike the earth with a curse.*

When families are not operational in the order of God, troubles and curses are released not only upon that family but into society as well. It is clear that the fatherlessness that is affecting our nation is the root problem to many of our struggles as a society. Our prisons are full, our children have no real identity, and people are aimless and seemingly lost, living only for the moment, and there are many other ills of society because of the lack of fathers within the family structure. As a result, our society is beset with curses that affect us all. Proverbs 3:33-35 tells us that the blessing of the Lord is on families in order while curses are on those who are not:

> *The curse of the Lord is on the house of the*
> *wicked,*

But He blesses the home of the just.
Surely He scorns the scornful,
But gives grace to the humble.
The wise shall inherit glory
But shame shall be the legacy of fools.

Whatever is upon our families will find its way into the whole of society. If a family is blessed because it is just, then that blessing will translate into the society that family is in. If a family is cursed because of wickedness, then that curse will find its way into society. Again, the family mountain has everything to do with the state of society and the reformation process. This is why the family mountain is the *values mountain*. The values of society flow from the family mountain. The family espouses and creates the values of society that afford us a foundation to function from. If this is eroded in the family, it is only a short time until society as a whole begins to crumble. This is why the psalmist asked the rhetorical question in Psalm 11:3:

If the foundations are destroyed,
What can the righteous do?

When foundations begin to be destroyed and even weakened, that which is built upon them will eventually fall. Because society's values flow from the family mountain there is an all-out attack against this sphere of influence. There are many enemies to the traditional family that want to change the core of what we believe to justify their immoral behavior and even to legitimize perversion and things the Lord clearly said were blights on society. We must continue the fight for the family mountain and the values of society that flow from it. I believe that the family/values mountain is of such importance because we can never sustain reformation in culture without it in a reformed state. Even if we were to magically set in place a fully reformed culture reflecting the kingdom of God, it could not be maintained without a family structure in godly order. In a very short time, whatever had been gained would be lost. This is why the devil is after the family. He understands this and so should we. We must fight to see the family mountain reformed and restored so godly *values* might again be reflected in our societies.

If we are going to see what the family mountain looks like in a reformed state, we should first understand the purpose of family. There are several purposes that family was created for by God. The first function of family was conquest. Most people think that family is first and foremost about companionship or fellowship. The reality is that God made family so that the progressive rule of the kingdom of God would impact the earth. The first family in scripture was made up of Adam, Eve, and then their children. Notice the commission that God gave to the first family. Genesis 1:26-28 tells us:

> *Then God said, "Let Us make man in Our image, according to Our likeness; let them have dominion over the fish of the sea, over the birds of the air, and over the cattle, over all the earth and over every creeping thing that creeps on the earth." So God created man in His own image; in the image of God He created him; male and female He created them. Then God blessed them, and God said to them, "Be fruitful and multiply; fill the earth and subdue it; have dominion over the fish of the sea, over the birds of the air, and over every living thing that moves on the earth."*

God's intent over family was always to expand the rule of His government throughout the earth. God took the man and eventually the woman and put them in the Garden of Eden. Even though He put them in the Garden, their commission was to the whole earth. They were to subdue it, take dominion over it, and — through fruitfulness and multiplication — rule over it. The Garden of Eden in that day was the *expression of the kingdom of God*. They were to take the expression of His kingdom and transplant it through the whole earth until all of the earth reflected His glory. God's agenda was always the whole of the earth. All the earth was to become a demonstration of His kingdom rule. This was to be done through family. In fact, when Adam was "alone" God said that this was not good (see Genesis 2:18). It was never said that Adam was lonely, only that he was alone. There is a difference. How could Adam have been lonely when he had never known companionship? Also, he was in complete and total unbroken fellowship and communion with the Father Himself. How could he be lonely?

God's purpose for forming Eve was not to heal loneliness in Adam—it was to create spiritual synergy for greater kingdom dominion in the earth. Remember that if one can put a thousand to flight then two can cause ten thousand to flee (see Deuteronomy 32:30). When God said it wasn't good for man to be alone, He was speaking of his kingdom influence into the earth. God made family for the purpose of conquest, not companionship. We can actually see this in the fact that before Eve was formed, Adam's realm was the garden. However, after her formation/creation *their* realm of authority became the world. Genesis 2:15 tells us that Adam's work was the Garden of Eden.

> *Then the Lord God took the man and put him in the garden of Eden to tend and keep it.*

We are then told that once Eve was joined to Adam, their domain became the earth. Genesis 1:27-28 lets us know that because of the synergy of the two being one they were to affect the whole world.

> *So God created man in His own image; in the image of God He created him; male and female He created them. Then God blessed them, and God said to them, "Be fruitful and multiply; fill the earth and subdue it; have dominion over the fish of the sea, over the birds of the air, and over every living thing that moves on the earth."*

Adam ruled the *garden,* but Adam and Eve were to rule the *earth.* We know the fall of man into sin interrupted this; however, it is still the plan of God. The purpose of family from the beginning was for conquest and the extension of the kingdom of God to the earth.

The devil stole away this idea and purpose from the family and made people think it was about them when it was really about God's purposes in the earth. Lest you think I believe that companionship is not important, it is impossible to have conquest without companionship. Real kingdom authority always flows out of proper community and companionship. Families must be in order for them to have the proper effect designed by God. This is why the devil fights so hard against the family mountain. As we have said, from this mountain there will be a great release of reformation and reformers who will carry the values of the kingdom of God and march forth with His passion. If the devil can disintegrate families from the inside out, then he can undo God's plan for dominion in the earth through the family mountain. Companionship and communion within family are absolute essentials to the conquest God intends. Husbands must love their wives, wives must honor their husbands, children must obey their parents, and life should be at peace within the ranks of the home. When this is present, we are then ready to execute the authority of God through the family and into the earth. The family's main purpose is the expansion of the rule of the kingdom of God in the earth.

Once the family understands that conquest is the agenda of God, then there is recognition of God's desire for the "godly seed." Scripture addresses the passion of the Lord for a "seed" of a godly nature to be released into the earth. Malachi 2:15 refers to the kind of children who will come from specific kinds of unions that will bring great effect into the societies of the earth:

> *But did He not make them one,*
> *Having a remnant of the Spirit?*
> *And why one?*
> *He seeks godly offspring.*
> *Therefore take heed to your spirit,*

And let none deal treacherously with the wife of his youth.

The Lord is after godly offspring or seed within the earth. Through this seed, the earth will be impacted with the rulership of God. We see the Lord going to great lengths to get this kind of seed into the earth. He sent angels and prophets to declare the birth of Josiah — the king who became a great reformer. Samson, spoken of before his birth by angels, set Israel free from bondage and slavery to alien nations. Even Jesus, the Seed of God Himself, was prophesied by prophets and angels for generations before His arrival to earth. From the family mountain, God will produce unions of marriage that will be holy from which the godly seed of reformers shall arise. In this verse from Malachi, the understanding is that when husbands and wives live together in right treatment of each other, godly seed is produced. The exhortation was that husbands and wives must guard their spirit so that they have a home conducive to raise the reformers God is after in the earth.

As the family begins to realize its real purpose in God, there will be an acceleration from generation to generation of blessings flowing down. We hear much today about family or generational curses. The only reason that family curses can operate is that they take advantage of the family lines that God created to carry blessings and anointings from generation to generation. Family lines are primarily to keep the blessing of God flowing down generational lines so there can be an increase in intensity and power. In fact, when we realize this we know that there is an exponential increase as this phenomenon occurs. The blessings, giftings, anointings, and powers that one generation carried and transferred to the next always should increase from generation to generation. We see this in the life of Timothy through his mother and grandmother. In II Timothy 1:5, Paul speaks of the faith that is in Timothy because it was first in his ancestors:

> *When I call to remembrance the genuine faith that is in you, which dwelt first in your grandmother Lois and your mother Eunice, and I am persuaded is in you also.*

Paul felt that the faith Timothy had toward the Lord was inherited from his mother and grandmother. It wasn't just something that he was taught; rather, it had been caught in the spirit from his family line. Timothy didn't start at ground zero when it came to faith. His power to believe was greatly strengthened because of the lineage he was drawing from. This is one of the purposes of family. We can *catch* spiritual blessings because of those who have gone before us and cultivated them for us. We don't have to do the work over again; we can simply step in to what they have done and take it further.

We see this within the authority of the kingdom being established in the earth. Daniel 4:3 shows us that the expansion of the kingdom rule of God into the earth is produced by generation synergy:

> *How great are His signs,*
> *And how mighty His wonders!*
> *His kingdom is an everlasting kingdom,*
> *And His dominion is from generation to*
> *generation.*

The kingdom rule of God is absolute. God Almighty is on His throne. Nothing can change this. Dominion is the literal enforcement of the kingdom into the earth, which is the job of generations. For this to happen progressively there must be the passing down of powers and authorities through family lines. As one generation works with the next generation, a synergy is created and a multiplication of anointing and gifts is released in the earth. We do not find ourselves starting over every generation but actually furthering the kingdom influence in the earth from generation to generation.

When this occurs, we have new levels of reformers who are being produced out of the family mountain to go into all the mountains and bring the revolution of the Lord to that sphere. It is impossible to see the reformation of society occur with prayer alone. We must have reformers produced who carry the sense of God's purpose and destiny in the depths of their spirits. We are seeing young people begin to come from homes to enter the mountains that the Lord has called them to. They are entering these mountains not just to make a living but to change the world. This is the heart of a reformer.

Proverbs 22:6 is a familiar scripture that many have misunderstood the ultimate meaning of:

> *Train up a child in the way he should go,*
> *And when he is old he will not depart from it.*

This scripture has commonly been spoken of as a source of comfort for a child who has been reared in a Christian home but has gone astray. This is quoted to usually say that they will return to the Lord even if it takes a long time and they are in their latter years. This may bring comfort and might even have some truth in it. But the real meaning of this scripture is to train a child up the *way he is bent*, and he will go that way. The idea is a tree that is planted when very small will grow with the *bend* that is in it. In other words, every child is born with a *bend* in them toward a calling of God for their lives. They are graced by God to do and accomplish certain things. It is the job of the parents to perceive that *bend* and help them go into one of the seven mountains that we have discussed. As the discernment is there concerning the mountain to which they are called, wise and understanding parents will help that child find their place in God in that mountain. When this occurs, we are going to see reformers by the thousands and even millions enter society and culture and begin to transform it. Children will be encouraged in their endeavors to go where God has prepared for them and see their ultimate purposes done as they fulfill the purpose of God for their lives.

Because we believe that people called into the business, media, government, or any other mountain are just as called as those called to the religion mountain or ministry, it is absolutely appropriate and essential for them to be commissioned into their calling. As young people come out of college or whatever training they need for their mountain, they should have hands laid on them with the prophetic and be *sent* into their sphere of work and ministry just like those in the religion mountain. As this begins to occur, the separation between the religion mountain and all the other mountains will fall. We will be empowering reformers to go into their mountain with the same impetus that has been used to send ministers into their mountain. When this happens, we are on our way to people not only having a career, but having a life to give to God's agenda in the earth.

CHAPTER 8

THE REFORMED FAMILY MOUNTAIN
Part 2: The Values Mountain

As reformers go into their mountain, they will begin to transform and reform the mountains of society. Remember that many of these reformers will have at least a portion of their roots in the family mountain. We must then know what this mountain looks like in a reformed state if we are to see its full effect being felt in society. There are seven characteristics of the family mountain in a reformed state.

The reformed family mountain will trumpet family values to a nation. A prophetic voice will be heard that establishes the values of the Lord in the earth. This prophetic voice must be fearless and without intimidation. If the foundation of family values is eroded then the nation that we love will cease to exist. The liberties that we have enjoyed for generations will be lost, and our children and grandchildren will experience a post-Christian nation that has lost its way.

There must be a trumpet sound from the family mountain that is full of the conviction of the Lord. This prophetic oracle must not be intimidated by being called outdated or out of touch with present realities. This is quite often the weapon of the LGBT agenda and those who want to label this prophetic sound as intolerant and even abusive. There is nothing further from the truth. Without this sound coming out of the reformed family mountain, our nation and the values that it is built on will be severely threatened and in danger of extinction.

Let me give an example of what I am speaking of in regard to a prophetic sound from the family mountain. Dr. James Dobson and the organizations/ministries he built has been one of these prophetic voices within our nation and the world. Through his sound and effort, there has been a restraining of the efforts by the god-less agendas to keep the traditional family values alive within our society. We must have these voices that herald the prophetic intent of God to a culture and society.

Matthew 5:11-12 gives us a picture of the fight that the prophetic voice of God has from this mountain. Again, those who are called to this battle must be absolutely fearless and committed to the cause:

Blessed are you when they revile and persecute you, and say all kinds of evil against you falsely for My sake. Rejoice and be exceedingly glad, for great is your reward in heaven, for so they persecuted the prophets who were before you.

When we stand up as a prophetic people into our generation to herald the cause of the Lord, there will be persecution that will arise. We are told that in these times we should rejoice because our reward is great in heaven. Those who take a stand with and for the Lord's purposes in the earth will be rewarded greatly. If they persecuted the prophets who were before us for their stand for the Lord, they will persecute those from the family mountain who are set to not give God's agenda away, but to fight for it to the death if necessary. This shall be greatly rewarded.

From the reformed family, great honor will flow into society because of the honor that is being learned at home. One of the greatest perils that we presently face is a society absent of honor. Our society is enraptured with shameless conduct and no real regard for authority. This seems to be what is applauded. The reason for this is the breakdown in the home. When children learn to respect and honor their father and mother in the home, it translates into every other aspect of society. But if that is not present in the home, then disdain and insubordination will be the norm in society as a whole. Ephesians 6:2-3 tells us the blessing, reward, and promise of the lessons of honor being learned in the family mountain:

> *"Honor your father and mother," which is the first commandment with promise: "that it may be well with you and you may live long on the earth."*

When honor is flowing in the home, people enter society with a sense of regard and esteem for every other part of God's creation. This results in a major difference being seen in almost all facets of society. Whether it is in the crime rate or the work force, people will act and respond differently. They will no longer live their lives with a sense of entitlement. It will no longer be about them but will be about others as well. This is the very spirit of Christ that is to be in the earth. When honor has been learned in the family mountain, not only will it bring the blessings of long life and things going well, but it will also affect how we relate and interact with our fellow man. Philippians 2:3-4 tells us that when this heart and awareness is in us from the home, we will not only think of ourselves but take into consideration the lives and feelings of others:

> *Let nothing be done through selfish ambition or conceit, but in lowliness of mind let each esteem*

others better than himself. Let each of you look out not only for his own interests, but also for the interests of others.

Honor always treats others the way they would want to be treated or even better.

As this element is released into society through the family mountain, fathers and mothers will begin again to hold the place of esteem that God designed. The ridicule that has been leveled at these places within our society will be stopped and we will have a family mountain espousing and setting the tone for honor in all of society. Not only will this honor release the blessing of the Lord into the home, but it will also be released into the whole of society as well. All of society will be transformed — if by nothing else, by the power of honor.

As the family mountain is brought into a place of reformation, children will become valued within our society as God intended. We have lost the value of children in society as a whole. They quite often are more seen as nuisances rather than treasures. As a result of this philosophy in society, the needs of children and even children themselves have been abused and mistreated. No wonder children are being raised with no real sense of self-worth or identity. These same children grow up to be dysfunctional adults and even menaces of society. Psalm 127:3-5 tells us the way God sees children and the way we are to see them as well:

> *Behold, children are a heritage from the Lord,*
> *The fruit of the womb is a reward.*
> *Like arrows in the hand of a warrior,*
> *So are the children of one's youth.*
> *Happy is the man who has his quiver full of*
> *them;*
> *They shall not be ashamed,*
> *But shall speak with their enemies in the gate.*

Children are the heritage of the Lord or His inheritance into the earth. They are His reward into our life. They are weapons of war designed to be shot forth into the earth to undo the enemy's influence and to bring reformation. The devil knows this so he works to make society devalue children and through selfishness and self-centeredness do hurt and harm to these whom God loves. This in reality is the root of abortion—a selfishness that values our own convenience above that which God puts such a high premium on that we are willing to kill them so our own lifestyles are not interrupted. As the family mountain is restored in the earth, this perspective will change, and children will once again hold the great place of nobility that was intended by God, and a generational way of thinking will be restored to society.

Other cultures and societies have had this way of thinking before us. I remember being in York, England gazing at the majesty of the York Minster. This is the building where the Church of England worships in that area. It is a magnificent piece of architecture. I became even more amazed when I was told that it took over 400 years to build. I realized that the plans, purpose, and passion for it had been passed from generation to generation until it was finished. Can you see something like this happening in our society today? I have a hard time imagining it because of our lack of generational thinking. Only when we begin to value children as God does will this kind of thing become a possibility. Even Hezekiah, the great king of restoration, struggled with having a generational heart. Isaiah 39:7-8 tells us that after Hezekiah had shown all the parts of his kingdom to the Babylonians, Isaiah the prophet confronted him and told him how foolish he had been:

> *"And they shall take away some of your sons who will descend from you, whom you will beget; and they shall be eunuchs in the palace of the king of Babylon."*
>
> *So Hezekiah said to Isaiah, "The word of the Lord which you have spoken is good!" For he said, "At least there will be peace and truth in my days."*

When told that some of his own children would become eunuchs who would be forced to serve the king of Babylon in captivity, Hezekiah's response was *that is a good word.* He said it was good because at least there would be peace in his days. What a selfish and self-seeking mentality that would have no heart for the coming generations or a heart for God's purposes in the earth. As we begin to value children the way God does, the reformation of the family mountain will be progressing.

As this mountain is reformed, there will also be a new sense of value placed upon the institution of marriage. No longer will marriage be something that is made fun of or even entered into lightly with the idea that if it doesn't work a divorce is the answer. There will be a sanctity connected to marriage once again. It will be seen as a covenant with God at the center rather than a convenience that will be maintained only until it isn't convenient anymore. Jesus tells us in Matthew 19:4-6 that we are not to separate what God has joined:

> *And He answered and said to them, "Have you not read that He who made them at the beginning 'made them male and female,' and said, 'For this reason a man shall leave his father and mother and be joined to his wife, and the two shall become one flesh'? So then, they are no longer*

two but one flesh. Therefore what God has joined together, let not man separate."

We are to return to the initial intent and purpose of the Lord. Divorce was only allowed because of a hardness of heart. As society becomes a picture of the kingdom of God, this will vanish away. We will return to the time when divorce was a humiliating thing that was avoided. The covenant and the pressure of society demanded that instead of running from the problems they were worked through. I have always said that covenant takes the back door out of marriage and makes us stand and deal with our marital struggles rather than fleeing from them through divorce.

Let me state that I do believe there are viable and biblical reasons for divorce. Ongoing adultery and betrayal, abuse, desertion, lack of support, and others that could be mentioned can constitute biblical reasons for divorce, but only after the last bit of resolve and effort has been spent to keep the marriage together. In the reformed family mountain, there will be a high commitment to marriage and its success in every situation.

There will also be a clear definition that marriage is the relationship between one man and one woman hopefully for one lifetime. Same-sex marriages, polygamy, and every other perversion will be debunked and destroyed by the traditional standards established and preserved from the family mountain.

From this place of reformation in the family mountain, children will grow up with a sense of stability and wellbeing as Dad and Mom love each other and the kids. This in itself will produce a great change in society because of the secured position that children have in a stable home.

The elderly will find a new esteem in the reformed mountain of family. Just like children, the value of our older citizens has waned. They are quite often seen as those who have used up their usefulness to the younger generation. Euthanasia is something that has become much more apparent in our society as this ideology has taken root. The prevailing thought has become to rid society of those who are no longer able to produce. What a godless thought pattern and worthy of all judgment. Leviticus 19:32 tells us the way the elderly are to be treated:

> You shall rise before the gray headed and honor
> the presence of an old man, and fear your God: I
> am the Lord.

The elderly are to be reverenced and honored out of the fear of God. God says that when we do this we are acknowledging that He is the Lord. In the reformed family mountain, there will be great honor for the elderly, the handicapped, the mentally challenged, and any other part of our society that is in need. As this is done from the family mountain, great lessons that are being lost will be passed on from generation to generation. As this begins to occur, it will be apparent that society is returning to the traditional family values and our nation is being refashioned by God's standards.

Very closely related to honoring the elderly is caring for widows. The primary care for widows is to flow from the family mountain. First Timothy 5:3-4 and 8 tell us that the ministry to widows in their need is not the government's job or the church's job, but rather the family's job:

> *Honor widows who are really widows. But if any widow has children or grandchildren, let them first learn to show piety at home and to repay their parents; for this is good and acceptable before God.*
>
> *...But if anyone does not provide for his own, and especially for those of his household, he has denied the faith and is worse than an unbeliever.*

Children and grandchildren are to take care of widows who are in need. We are to see to it that their needs are met. When we do this, we are repaying them for taking care of us in our growing up years. As the family mountain is restored, the nuclear family will begin to see this as their job and responsibility. There will not be a setting aside in nursing homes for convenience's sake. There will be a loving and caring family that will operate together with multiple generations under one roof where necessary. Again, we will see the spirit of selfishness dismantled and removed as the mountain of family is reformed.

A final thought on the family mountain being reformed is that it will heal many social ills as the family is put squarely back upon its foundation. First Timothy 5:16 gives us some insight into what happens as the family takes its place in God's plan for society:

> *If any believing man or woman has widows, let them relieve them, and do not let the church be burdened, that it may relieve those who are really widows.*

Notice that as family takes care of its own, it relieves the church and other structures of that responsibility. The church as well as government is freed from the responsibility for certain people in our society when the family is functioning in its God-ordained order. One of the reasons for such pressure on the church and government is because the family has been so out of order. As this is restored and reformed, the pressure on other entities will be eased because the family is stepping up and helping and caring for those who are theirs.

What a wonderful plan God has arranged. The reformed family mountain will affect all of society and press us forward to a true demonstration of God's kingdom on planet earth. It will reestablish the values that have been thrown away so that the blessings of God can begin to legally flow back into society. God will use the family mountain to shape the values of society in this generation and the ones to come.

PRAYER POINTS
for the Courts of Heaven

1. Pray for revelation of the importance of this mountain to the value system of society.

2. Pray for courage and fearlessness in those called to this mountain.

3. Pray against the redefining of the family and for a return to traditional family values.

4. Pray for reformers who carry godly values to be produced from this mountain for all the mountains.

5. Pray for a generational heart to be developed that sees beyond the immediate and into the future.

As we come before Your Courts, Lord, we petition You concerning the family mountain. We ask for a restoration of this mountain and sphere of influence. Only as this mountain is reformed can we see sustained reformation into culture.

I ask first, Lord, that there would be a revelation of the importance of this mountain in culture. Forgive us for dismissing family as irrelevant and unimportant. We repent for this gross misjudgment and all the results of it. Let Your Blood, Jesus, please speak for us according to Hebrews 12:24. Allow a fresh understanding and a fresh emphasis to now come upon us concerning family and its place in Your heart and desires.

I ask also that there would be reformers raised who would carry deep longings in their hearts for social family reformation. May they stand as a prophetic voice into our culture with great courage. May they have the right spirit within them that will allow an uncompromising sound to exude for the reclaiming of this mountain.

As I stand before Your Courts, I also request that there would be a judgment against anything that would redefine what family is. Would You allow a judgment to be rendered from Your Courts against anything that would pervert Your definition of family. Let every perversion fall and the true manifestation of family be revealed.

Lord, I also request that alongside the religion mountain and the education mountain, reformers would arise from the family mountain. Let the godly seed/offspring come from the family mountain that would have great impact in our nations. Lord, cause deliverers to arise that will reorder culture and society.

And finally, Lord, I petition Your Courts that a generational heart would develop in Your people and even in society as a whole. Let us not be preoccupied with only our time and space. Give us a heart that will impregnate our children and grandchildren and beyond with a generational mindset. Allow this, I pray, that Your plan and purpose might proceed from generation to generation.

Thank You so much, Lord. May we be heard and esteemed as we stand before Your Courts of Heaven, in Jesus' Name, amen.

CHAPTER 9

THE REFORMED EDUCATION MOUNTAIN
Part 1: The Equipping Mountain

The mountain of education is the third of the three mountains from which reformers will come for all the mountains. When the family, religion, and education mountains are in full operation, there will be a sending forth of reformers into all the mountains of society. Society will be altered and reformed through the prayer of God's people and the reformers being sent into their God-called mountain. When God created the earth in Genesis, He commanded that every plant had its seed within it. In other words, the seed brought forth of its own kind. Genesis 1:11 tells us that the seed determines what was produced:

> *Then God said, "Let the earth bring forth grass, the herb that yields seed, and the fruit tree that*

> *yields fruit according to its kind, whose seed is in*
> *itself, on the earth"; and it was so.*

Reformers will be the seed of reformation that goes forth into their given mountain to produce after their own kind. We are developing seeds of reformation that have the effect of reformation in their place of function in the earth. We must have the right seed or reformer to give birth to the kind of reformation we are after. From the religion mountain, the divine sense of destiny for reformation will be produced in these seeds, which will create the impetus or driving force of reformation. From the family mountain, the values necessary for reformation will be imparted. This will keep all things on track. The education mountain will bring the third piece, which is the equipping element. Therefore, the education mountain is the *equipping mountain*. Equipping with the necessary information, intellectual abilities, realms of thinking, and skills to communicate effectively flows from this mountain. If we are to reform society, we must be equipped and even skilled in the ways that the world responds to. We must have great thinkers who can communicate our positions in such a way that society will listen, understand, and embrace.

Daniel and his friends were all trained in the ways of the Babylonians (see Daniel 1:3-4). As a result, they were able to take the training and skill they had used and, without compromise to their spiritual convictions, mix it with the supernatural and reform a kingdom. Their influence within that sphere flowed from the sense of divine appointment that came from the religion mountain, a sense of the values of the Lord that flowed from their upbringing in the home or the family mountain, but also from the training and equipping they received in the education mountain of their day. This was what made them such great reformers.

They would not have been who they were without all three of these spheres having input and impact on their lives. As great as the sense of destiny is from the religion mountain and the foundation of values is from the family mountain, without the equipping of the education mountain, reformation would not have occurred. The education mountain releases into society the equipping necessary to empower reformers and reformation. Reformation cannot happen without this equipping. We must therefore see the education mountain come into the reformed state necessary to impact reformers and society. Education is necessary to everything we do.

Without education, people will be subject to tyranny and oppression. This has been proven over and over throughout the generations. When people are uneducated, they will be ruled over by those who are educated. The Reformation that was born through Martin Luther progressed and was thrust forward through the education of the masses. Up until that time, only the religious hierarchy had the ability to read the scriptures and then tell the people what they said and how they were to be interpreted. This placed the masses of people into a dependence on many who were unrighteous and self-serving in their interpretation of the scriptures.

When Luther arose and nailed his theses to the door as an act of rebellion toward what was holding people in bondage, the Reformation began. The whole doctrine of justification through faith came forth, and people began to be brought out from under the bondage of the educated. The reformation of Luther was the first to utilize the printing press on a large scale. They began to get literature out that educated the people of their day so that the tyranny of the educated over the uneducated could be broken. The result was that the church founded schools and universities. They became the civilizer and instructor of the barbarians of that age. As the printing press found its use in the Reformation, it gave a powerful impulse and drive to common schools. Protestantism favored the general diffusion of knowledge, as opposed to the Catholic Church of that day restricting it to a few. As a result, the laity was emancipated to private judgment and stimulated to a sense of personal responsibility. They no longer were dependent on the priests of their day making atonement for them with the money they were told they must give. People began to understand that salvation was a personal matter resulting from an active faith in the atoning work of Jesus on the cross.

Much of this was the result of the printed word being brought to the common person and educational systems being established out of Protestantism. In other words, the Catholic Church of that day preyed on the ignorance of the common people and their lack of education. On the other hand, Protestantism empowered the common person with education and liberated and stimulated them with knowledge.

It is the same today. If we are to see a turn in society and another great reformation occur, we must influence and gain control of the educational systems of our day. This mountain has to be reclaimed and reformed back to the kingdom of God. There must be an invasion into this mountain of prayer power and reformers if we are to see this mountain begin to reflect and influence society as a kingdom entity.

If we are to see this happen, we must first understand the goals and purposes of education and its system. Remember that everything has a purpose, and the first step toward a reformation of anything is to begin to recognize the purpose of that thing.

As we have already discussed, education is first and foremost a liberator. When people become educated, they can then make decisions for themselves as informed people rather than depending upon what someone else is telling them. The devil clearly uses ignorance to exploit people and hold them in bondage. Second Corinthians 2:11 tells us that satan seeks to get an advantage over us through ignorance:

> *Lest Satan should take advantage of us; for we are not ignorant of his devices.*

Ignorance has been used by evil people and forces throughout the ages to work their diabolical plans. When people become educated they then are empowered to break free from the yokes that have been thrust on their necks through ignorance. Francis Bacon's comment on men and their thoughts toward education are revealing: "Crafty men condemn studies, simple men admire them, and wise men use them."[1]

The crafty condemn education because it works against their agenda. Others see the benefit of being educated and employ it. The Lord is very clear in His word that lack of knowledge can actually bring about destruction. The first portion of Hosea 4:6 shows this truth:

My people are destroyed for lack of knowledge.

As people are educated in the reformed mountain of education, there will be great empowerment that is released to every level of society. Some of the deception that society now lives under by the rhetoric of liberal thinkers will be debunked because people are learning by education to think for themselves. One of the greatest weapons of the devil against any people is ignorance, but one of the greatest assets in the arsenal of God is education. Education equips us to live life in freedom and power.

As people become educated, there will also be an ignition in the soul. William Butler Yeats said, "Education is not the filling of a pail, but the lighting of a fire."[2] Education is not about the acquiring of information, facts, or even knowledge. Education is about igniting the soul with a passion to accomplish something yet undone. When education is reduced to a simple learning of facts, equations, or other mundane interests, all that has been done is inoculating people against any real passion for life. Through education there must be a forming of a reformer's heart and a stirring of passion with a fire that can never be quenched. When this is done, then education has reached it utmost pinnacle.

Education is also to bring discernment. A.W. Tozer pointed out, "Perception of ideas rather than the storing of them should be the aim of education. The mind should be an eye to see with rather than a bin to store facts in. The man who has been taught by the Holy Spirit will be a seer rather than a scholar. The difference is that the scholar sees and the seer sees through; and that is a mighty difference indeed."[3]

What a profound insight and statement about the purpose of education. Our mind should be an eye to see rather than a bin to store facts. We should be seers rather than scholars as a result of education, and the difference is not just to see, but to *see through* or to discern. Through education, the mind is trained to perceive and think things through rather than just store facts. When this is accomplished and we have developed thinkers and not just learners, the spirit of discernment is released. Philippians 1:9-10 tells us that abounding in knowledge and discernment is essential to us being able to put our stamp of approval on things:

> *And this I pray, that your love may abound still more and more in knowledge and all discernment, that you may approve the things that are excellent, that you may be sincere and without offense till the day of Christ.*

How often have we verified things and then later found out that they were not what we thought they were? As we become thinkers inspired by the Holy

Spirit, we will be able to really approve the things that are excellent. We will not be deceived and inadvertently place our approval on what God is not approving. A part of this is being educated to the point of not just learning, but thinking.

As we are progressively educated, we also stay young regardless of how old we are. An anonymous person once said, "Anyone who stops learning is old, whether at twenty or eighty."[4] There is something about the desire to learn that keeps us young. Through learning, we constantly refresh not just our mind but our spirit and inner man as well. This stimulation causes our spirit to be alive. Second Corinthians 4:16 tells us that even though we are aging in our bodies, our spirit can be renewed and alive:

> *Therefore we do not lose heart. Even though our outward man is perishing, yet the inward man is being renewed day by day.*

One of the best pictures of this is the eagle. We are told that as we wait on and minister to the Lord, our youth is renewed like the eagle's (see Isaiah 40:31). We will mount up on the wings of eagles as we catch the wind currents and soar to unbelievable heights. We will run with vision and not grow weary. We will walk out the purposes of God and not faint. This is because we have learned the secrets of a young heart. A part of

this process is a renewing of the mind through education. We must never stop learning but always keep our
mind alert and engaged.

Through education, the coming generations will be
fashioned. Liberal thinking and godless agendas have
polluted the education mountain, and as a result we
have lost several generations for kingdom purposes. As
the mountain of education is reclaimed, a big purpose
of education will be realized as we raise fearless young
people who will produce a revolution that results in a
reformation. Psalm 78:5-8 tells us that if we don't want
a repeat of what has been, we must affect the coming
generation with the word of God and right education.

> *For He established a testimony in Jacob,*
> *And appointed a law in Israel,*
> *Which He commanded our fathers,*
> *That they should make them known to their*
> *children;*
> *That the generation to come might know them,*
> *The children who would be born,*
> *That they may arise and declare them to their*
> *children,*
> *That they may set their hope in God,*
> *And not forget the works of God,*
> *But keep His commandments;*
> *And may not be like their fathers,*

A stubborn and rebellious generation,
A generation that did not set its heart aright,
And whose spirit was not faithful to God.

Notice that the purpose of this generational impact was so that they could *not be like their fathers*. If we are going to change society, we must reclaim what the fathers have lost. This requires that the coming generations not fall under the same influence that we have but that they are moved under another influence of kingdom perspective. This will require a reformation of the mountain of education. Without the reformation of this sphere, we will never see society change and begin to reflect the glories of God's kingdom here in earth. Such is the power of this mountain of education.

Alexander Pope, speaking about the effect of education on the mind of any person, but especially a young person, said, "Tis education forms the common mind, as the twig is bent the tree's inclined."[5] The power of education to form the thinking of a person is like the bending of a twig.

Whichever way a twig is bent, the tree will grow to be. Picture a mighty oak that is swayed a certain way. The reason for its sway is because it was bent that way as a twig. There are many mighty oaks in the coming generations. We must have the right educational process to bend them the way of the kingdom if we are to reclaim the societies of the earth.

Sydney J. Harris spoke of the purpose of education: "Most people are mirrors, merely reflecting the mood and emotions of the times; few are windows, bringing light to bear on the dark corners, where troubles fester; and the whole purpose of education is to turn mirrors into windows."[6] We don't need mirrors just reflecting back to us the problems we already are aware of. We need windows that can bring light into a dark situation and transform it from a problem to a paradise. Windows are reformers who are being created out of the educational mountain and come forth with a fire and lightning in their souls to reform the mountain that God has called them into.

Notes

1. Edythe Draper, ed. *Draper's Book of Quotations for the Christian World* (Wheaton, IL: Tyndale House, 1992), 2996.

2. Ibid., 3002.

3. Ibid., 3021.

4. Ibid., 2995.

5. Ibid., 2991.

6. Ibid., 3019.

CHAPTER 10

THE REFORMED EDUCATION MOUNTAIN
Part 2: The Equipping Mountain

As the mountain of education is reformed, it will have several trademarks and characteristics about it. From a prophetic viewpoint, this is what I see the education mountain looking like in a reformed state.

The reformed education mountain will impart not just facts but morality as well. Young people who have the power to reform society will need a moral compass about them. First Timothy 1:19 shows us what happens when there is no moral compass in the hearts of people:

> *Having faith and a good conscience, which some having rejected, concerning the faith have suffered shipwreck.*

A shipwrecked state is the result of someone who has steered off course. The compass that keeps people on course is faith and a good conscience. If either of these is not operating, people will end up with their lives, destiny, and purpose on the rocks. In the present educational system, people are taught no real sense of morality. Humanism says there is no absolute truth. When this is believed and embraced, it leads to a place of darkness and futility. Romans 1:21 tells us what happens when we expel God from any educational process of the mind:

> *Because, although they knew God, they did not glorify Him as God, nor were thankful, but became futile in their thoughts, and their foolish hearts were darkened.*

Without God and His ways at the center of the educational process, people's hearts, thoughts, minds, and intellect become darkened and foolish. All sorts of demonic ideas start to arise out of the power of the soul that have no moral compass attached to them. Noah Webster said, "Education is useless without the Bible."[1]

The Bible is the source of the moral absolutes of our existence. When it is not adhered to or reverenced as God's word to us, education becomes useless and even works against society. We can become like those who through wisdom do not know or recognize God (see I Corinthians 1:21). As my mother often said, we become "too big for our britches." We think we are wise and smart but have left the foundation that has the power to make us great.

C.S. Lewis in his attempt to articulate the need for the involvement of religion in education said, "Education without religion, as useful as it is, seems rather to make man a more clever devil."[2] His conclusion was that educated people who have no real moral compass quite often become more devilish in their influence into society than the uneducated would be. We must shoot for the morality of who God is to be in the education mountain. The ultimate goal would be for the gospel of Jesus Christ to be at the center of the education mountain. This may happen in some institutions, but it may not in most or all. I would suggest that the reformed mountain of education would not have an outright declaration of Jesus Christ at its core, but rather a commitment to morality that flows from the virtue of Jesus Himself.

Charles Habib Malik suggests this same concept, "So far as the university is concerned, I have no patience with piety alone—I want the most rigorous intellectual training, I want the perfection of the mind; equally, I have no patience with reason alone—I want the salvation of the soul, I want the fear of the Lord, I want at least neutrality with respect to the knowledge of Jesus Christ."[3]

Obviously from our Christian viewpoint, we would want the Lord Jesus Christ to be at the center of the educational process. This is what Malik is communicating. But in the absence of it, he is requesting that there would at least be a neutrality toward the Lord Jesus and who He is. In other words, there would not be outright antagonism, attacking of beliefs, and the antichrist spirit and godless agenda within the system. There would be a commitment to godly standards regardless of where people supposed they originated. Within this system would be the freedom to educate and place within the hands the weapons that our young people would use to change society. Otherwise, we place within their hands bombs used to destroy society when education is administered with no moral compass. We end up empowering the old nature of man, who is corrupt in all his ways, rather than empowering a people who have the betterment of society in their hearts.

As the mountain of education is reformed, an unlocking of potential in the ones who are being educated will occur. So often what we have had is the making of bricks rather than the fashioning of stones. Scripture tells us about the construction of the tower of Babel. This was an ungodly attempt to make for themselves a name and to exalt themselves and their agenda in the earth. We see in Genesis 11:3 that they chose to use *baked bricks* for this endeavor:

> *Then they said to one another, "Come, let us make bricks and bake them thoroughly." They had brick for stone, and they had asphalt for mortar.*

Stones speak of the individuality of a person. Baked bricks speak of uniformity and control and of being indoctrinated and told what to think rather than how to think. This has been primarily how the present educational system has functioned. They have produced baked bricks to promote their anti-God agendas. If we are going to reform the education mountain, it will have a release of creativity in it. Sydney J. Harris said, "The best teacher is not one who crams the most into a pupil, but who gets the most out of one. Education is a process not of stuffing people, like sausage into a casing, but of eliciting from people the potentialities hidden even from themselves."[4]

We are not to be making bricks by stuffing students with information, agendas, and rhetoric. We are to be unlocking them so that what is in them from a creative standpoint can begin to flow out. There is a reformer in every person on some level. We must have educational systems that pull that reformer out. The right stuff on the inside of folks can be pulled out to answer many

IMPACTING THE SEVEN MOUNTAINS *from the* COURTS OF HEAVEN

of society's woes and ills. If we will quit stuffing them and start pulling out the right stuff, we will find the answers from God for many of our present problems.

As the education mountain comes into a reformed state, there will be a longing for wisdom and knowledge that will be imparted to those being educated. It will take this longing for reformers to move forward from this mountain. Proverbs 15:2 tells us that wisdom is the right use of knowledge—we are not only to be imparting knowledge but the wisdom to use that knowledge rightly as well:

> *The tongue of the wise uses knowledge rightly,*
> *But the mouth of fools pours forth foolishness.*

Clearly the wise know how to use the knowledge that is theirs. In the midst of getting knowledge, there must also be the impartation of wisdom as well. Proverbs 4:7 tells us that wisdom is more important than knowledge:

> *Wisdom is the principal thing;*
> *Therefore get wisdom.*
> *And in all your getting, get understanding.*

When educational systems simply impart knowledge and do not create an atmosphere for wisdom to be introduced, a great injustice has been committed.

We must have the wisdom to know how to use the knowledge we have appropriately. I think that Sydney J. Harris espouses this very nicely: "The most worthwhile form of education is the kind that puts the educator inside you, as it were, so that the appetite for learning persists long after the external pressure for grades and degrees has vanished. Otherwise you are not educated; you are merely trained."[5]

We do not want just trained individuals. We must have truly educated people who carry a passion from the inside to know more perfectly how to take the knowledge they have and apply it into life. This requires the "educator" to be internal. There must be an appetite for learning that persists so that the application of what is known can change the world we live in. When this happens, a person who has really been empowered results.

As this mountain is reformed, there will also be an impartation of self-worth that flows from the educational process. Most of our youth come out of their educational process with no real identity or sense of purpose. Could this be because they are being told that they come from apes and are just evolved animals? Why are we surprised when our young people act like animals and have no sense of respect for human life? They know only to follow their base instincts rather than live up to the standard of being fashioned in the image of a loving God. Genesis 1:27 tells us that all of us are made in the image of God, not an evolved animal:

> *So God created man in His own image; in the image of God He created him; male and female He created them.*

When this is communicated instead of the other philosophy, this in itself has the power to lift us up into a new awareness of who we are. When young people have a low or no self-image and sense of self-worth, they sell out cheaply. Proverbs 20:14 shows us one of the ploys of the devil to persuade people to go his way rather than the way planned by God for them:

> *"It is good for nothing," cries the buyer;*
> *But when he has gone his way, then he boasts.*

The devil convinces and tells people that they are good for nothing so they will sell out cheaply. This is easy to do when our educational system reinforces the whole idea of worthlessness.

If we are going to reform the education mountain, at its core must be the persuasion of who our young people are and the power they carry within them. When this is in them, they will live up to who they understand and believe themselves to be. Pablo Casal states this principle very well:

> When will we teach our children in school what they are? We should say to each of them: Do you know what you are? You are a marvel. You are unique. In all of the world there is no other child exactly like you. In the millions of years that have passed there has never been another child like you. And look at your body — what a wonder it is! Your legs, your arms, your cunning fingers, the way you move! You may become a Shakespeare, a Michelangelo, a Beethoven. You have the capacity for anything. Yes, you are a marvel. And when you grow up, can you then harm another who is, like you, a marvel?[6]

When a sense of self-worth is established, a deep sense of the sacredness of life will follow. As this becomes a part of the educational process, we will unlock potential that has long been hindered. Our young people will come forth with planet-altering expectations and the ability to perform them. The power of who and what we think ourselves to be is bigger than any of us can imagine or consider — it unlocks capacities that are unimaginable.

The reformed education mountain will also produce great minds. If we are going to reform society, we must have great minds that the world will listen to. As the

Lord spoke to His people, He said they were to carry such great wisdom that nations would listen to them and want to know their secrets. Deuteronomy 4:6-7 tells us that as they obeyed the Lord, other nations would recognize the closeness of God to them and the wisdom with which they operated:

> *Therefore be careful to observe them; for this is your wisdom and your understanding in the sight of the peoples who will hear all these statutes, and say, "Surely this great nation is a wise and understanding people." For what great nation is there that has God so near to it, as the Lord our God is to us, for whatever reason we may call upon Him?*

We must have great minds that the world recognizes within our ranks. Charles Habib Malik saw this need as well:

> Who among the evangelicals can stand up to the great secular or naturalistic or atheistic scholars on their own terms of scholarship and research? Who among the evangelical scholars is quoted as a normative source by the greatest secular authorities on history or philosophy or psychology or sociology or politics? Does your mode of thinking

> have the slightest chance of becoming the
> dominant mode of thinking in the great
> universities of Europe and America which
> stamp your entire civilization with their
> own spirit and ideas?[7]

Notice that he wondered whether our mode of thinking could become the dominant realm in universities of Europe and America. The point being that we must have great minds as well as spirituality if we have any hope of reforming this mountain of education. This means that the church has to change its philosophy and begin to put a premium not just on the spiritual dimension but the intellectual one as well. We are to have the wisdom that the world would clamor to our door to hear. David understood this as a secular king of Israel. He said in Psalm 119:98-100 that he was wiser than his enemies and even the ancients—he had a superior mental, intellectual, and spiritual dimension:

You, through Your commandments, make me
wiser than my enemies;
For they are ever with me.
I have more understanding than all my teachers,
For Your testimonies are my meditation.
I understand more than the ancients,
Because I keep Your precepts.

David said he was wiser than his enemies, his teachers, and the ancients because of the effects of the word of God on his life. This should be true for us as well. Mental capabilities do not flow out of the mind but the spirit empowered by the word of God. Yet we must be able to take concepts from the spiritual dimension of our lives and communicate them without sounding like religious freaks. We must be able to release kingdom principles into society from superior mental capacities without quoting scripture if we desire to impact society.

As the mountain of education is reformed, there will be great minds aroused that have the ability to debate the godless into submission. They will come up with answers for disease, troubles, and problems that seem to have no answers because of the empowerment of God within their mental abilities. The reformed education mountain will be a breeding ground for such.

As alluded to previously, one of the main attributes of a reformed education mountain will be the production of reformers into society. The religion mountain will espouse the agenda of destiny, the family mountain will establish the value system, and the education mountain will equip the heart, soul, and mind. As this is accomplished, a release of reformers will come forth into the earth. There will be reformers thrust forth from these mountains just as David was in his generation.

Acts 13:36 tells us that David served his generation and accomplished God's will as a reformer before he died:

For David, after he had served his own gener-ation by the will of God, fell asleep, was buried with his fathers, and saw corruption.

The life of David counted as a reformer. He lived his life and accomplished what was appointed by God for him to do. There will be many reformers who shall come out of the reformed mountain of education. Joseph Addison shows the aspiration of education to produce these people of renown, impact, and reforma-tion: "What sculpture is to a block of marble, education is to the human soul. The philosopher, the saint, the hero, the wise and the good, or the great, very often lie hid and concealed in a plebeian, which a proper edu-cation might have disinterred and brought to light."[8]

When the mountain of education is reformed, it will act as a sculptor in uncovering the greatness that lies in our youth. A proper education will bring it to light, and the world will never be the same again. This is the education mountain *being* the equipping mountain — preparing and releasing reformers into society. Let us pray, work, motivate, and exhort until this mountain is reformed and begins to reflect the splendors of God's kingdom and rule in the earth. The earth will never be the same, and life on the planet will be altered forever.

NOTES

1. Draper, *Draper's Book of Quotations,* 3003.
2. Ibid., 3005
3. Ibid., 3025
4. Ibid., 3026
5. Ibid., 3031
6. Ibid., 3039.
7. Ibid., 3040.
8. Ibid., 3038.

PRAYER POINTS
for the Courts of Heaven

1. Pray for an awareness of the impact of education on reformation.

2. Pray for the church to value education alongside spirituality.

3. Pray for educators to be produced and placed to transform educational systems.

4. Pray for morality to accompany the educational process.

5. Pray for reformers to enter society equipped for reformation from the educational mountain.

As I approach Your Courts, Lord, I stand for the education mountain and Your purposes in it. I repent for what we have allowed this mountain to become. We have allowed it to be a spring of godlessness and ruled by the antichrist spirit. I ask that here might be a judgment from Your Courts against this spirit. Let the education mountain be freed, I pray, from this influence. Let it again be a source of fulfilling Your purposes in the earth.

I pray, Lord, and petition Your Courts that a new awareness would come to the church of the importance of education. May we repent for any dismissing of education for spirituality. May we know that the two can flow together.

I pray that we would maintain a high esteem for spiritual matters. However, allow us to value education. Forgive us for not imparting this to our children in a proper manner.

I also petition these Courts that there might be educators raised who would transform the present educational systems. Let people of courage and faith take a stand. May there be those on whom You have placed Your hand who can alter this system that it might help Your kingdom process and not hinder it.

I also request that there would be a new morality emphasis that would be coupled with education. May our schools and universities espouse the need for morality and righteous standards alongside educational processes.

Lord, I ask that You might allow reformers to be prepared and enter this mountain. Allow that from the religion, family, and now education mountains, reformers would flow forth to change not just the education mountain but also culture and society as a whole. We are desperate for Your help and intervention, Lord. May Your divine purposes be done and may our societies become expressions of Your kingdom. In Jesus' Name, amen.

CHAPTER 11

THE REFORMED GOVERNMENT MOUNTAIN
Part 1: The Empowering Mountain

No other mountain directly affects our lives more than the mountain of government. When I speak of government, I am not speaking of politics. Politics may be the realm in which we elect those who function in government, but politics is not government. God is government Himself. Government is the exercising of authority for the purpose of order within the earth that produces a protection and empowering of society. Therefore, the government mountain is the *empowering mountain*.

All authority comes from the Lord. Matthew 28:18 tells us that all authority has rightfully been given to Jesus in heaven above and in earth below:

> *And Jesus came and spoke to them, saying, "All authority has been given to Me in heaven and on earth."*

When Jesus died on the cross, was placed into the grave, descended into hell, and then arose to ascend to His place at the right hand of the Father, all authority in every dimension became His. He now delegates portions of the authority He carries to people to bring order and empowerment to the earth. This is why Romans 13:1-2 tells us that no one operating in governmental authority has it except that God gave it:

> *Let every soul be subject to the governing authorities. For there is no authority except from God, and the authorities that exist are appointed by God. Therefore whoever resists the authority resists the ordinance of God, and those who resist will bring judgment on themselves.*

This is the reason we must honor, respect, and adhere to, as much as we can, the governmental authorities of our world. We also have the right and privilege to reform the government mountain. This allows the righteous decrees of the Lord to go forth and reflect His heart. Isaiah 9:6-7 shows us that every government of this earth is upon the shoulders of Jesus, because He carries all authority, right, and power:

For unto us a Child is born,
Unto us a Son is given;
And the government will be upon His shoulder.
And His name will be called
Wonderful, Counselor, Mighty God,
Everlasting Father, Prince of Peace.
Of the increase of His government and peace
There will be no end,
Upon the throne of David and over His
kingdom,
To order it and establish it with judgment and
justice
From that time forward, even forever.
The zeal of the Lord of hosts will perform this.

From the time of Jesus' entrance into the earth, the kingdom of God has come. This is why there will be no end to the increase of His government and peace. This is also why every government in the earth must be targeted with reformation. The government mountain must be reformed like no other. Without reformation, the devil uses this mountain to release his agenda into the earth. This mountain is a gate that is used in a massive way to alter society and its function. We must possess this gate if the kingdom of God is going to make massive inroads into society. Authority by nature exercises influence over society through legislative acts, judicial decisions, and executive orders. If the people occupying these places of government or authority are warped in their thinking as it relates to God's agenda in the earth, then the forces of satan use them to oppose God's purposes in society. They become a channel for his evil intents to operate through. We must have reformers produced who hold these places of decision-making. When they do, they become a channel for God's agenda in government rather than satan's. When things are in order, the mountain of government becomes this *empowering mountain*.

The government mountain includes several different spheres. It includes local, state, and national expressions of government. It includes laws and policy. It includes lobbyists, ambassadors, social services, military, police, and civil service. Any interaction within these areas means we are functioning within the government mountain. It is impossible to be involved in realms of life and not be affected by the government mountain. All of us are touched by it in one form or the other. Decisions made and the enforcement of those decisions touch us all. This is one of the reasons we must see this mountain brought into a reformed state. The main reason, though, is so that what God wants in the earth may be realized.

To see reformation come, a great sense of morality and justice must be established at the core of this mountain. The kingdom or government of Solomon is probably one of the clearest pictures of a government that reflects what God desires. As the Queen of Sheba came to visit Solomon to examine his kingdom and the function of it in the earth, she was astounded. She proclaimed that because God loved Israel, He had made Solomon king over this nation. First Kings 10:9 records the words of this ruler herself:

> *Blessed be the Lord your God, who delighted in you, setting you on the throne of Israel! Because the Lord has loved Israel forever, therefore He made you king, to do justice and righteousness.*

She realized that the function of government was to administer the justice of the Lord into the earth. When government is functioning properly, the justice and righteousness of the Lord Himself will flow out of that government to the people. Psalm 89:14 tells us that God's own throne has foundations under it of righteousness and justice. Whatever is the stabilizing force of the throne of God will be the stabilizing effect of any throne or government here on earth:

> *Righteousness and justice are the foundation of Your throne;*
> *Mercy and truth go before Your face.*

When a government is committed to righteousness and justice for all people in the earth, that government will be reflecting the government of God Himself.

This is why there can be no partiality within government. The corruptness of government can be traced back to partiality shown for favors promised. In the end, this almost always involves monetary benefit. This was always strictly forbidden by God in any of His people who would function in a governmental place. Deuteronomy 1:16-17 is one of the places where God disallows any form of partiality to work among His governmental officials:

> *Then I commanded your judges at that time, saying, "Hear the cases between your brethren, and judge righteously between a man and his brother or the stranger who is with him. You shall not show partiality in judgment; you shall hear the small as well as the great; you shall not be afraid in any man's presence, for the judgment is God's. The case that is too hard for you, bring to me, and I will hear it."*

Moses commanded those who were entrusted with the making of judicial decisions to be righteous and just no matter what person they were dealing with. Whether the individuals were important or not did not matter. The judgments rendered had to be without partiality and favor.

The founding fathers of America understood how important this was to a government like democracy. John Adams, the second President of the United States, declared that only a people committed to moral absolutes and righteousness of heart could have a government such as democracy operate: "We have no government armed in power capable of contending with human passions unbridled by morality and religion...Our constitution was made only for a moral and religious people. It is wholly inadequate for the government of any other."[1]

The government that operates must have moral absolutes from which judgments are rendered and righteousness is required. Otherwise there will be a falling into a partiality brought on by the bribes of lobbyists and other people of agenda. This has been so present within the government mountain that even our leaders have spoken of it. President Theodore Roosevelt said, "When they call the roll in the Senate, the senators do not know whether to answer 'present' or 'not guilty.'"[2]

The truth is that power corrupts and absolute power corrupts absolutely. We must have a new breed of governmental people whose hearts are set on reforming the government mountain. Instead of politicians, we need statesmen who can carry forth the agenda of God, which is a government that ministers to all the people and not just a few.

As the mountain of government is reformed, it will provide peace for life, protection for society, and empowerment living. This is a major purpose for government in the earth. Wherever you see government mentioned in the scripture, you see peace mentioned or implied. Notice Isaiah 9:7 speaking of the government of Jesus Himself:

> *Of the increase of His government and peace*
> *There will be no end,*
> *Upon the throne of David and over His kingdom,*
> *To order it and establish it with judgment and justice*
> *From that time forward, even forever.*
> *The zeal of the Lord of hosts will perform this.*

The yoking together of righteous government and peace is declared. The purpose of government is to bring about order so that all people can live in peace. Scripture lifts up the government of Solomon as a picture of proper government and the canopy it provides for its citizens to live under. First Kings 4:25 tells us of the people of Israel and the kind of atmosphere they lived under during the reign of Solomon:

> *And Judah and Israel dwelt safely, each man under his vine and his fig tree, from Dan as far as Beersheba, all the days of Solomon.*

Each man was under his own vine and his own fig tree. There was no intrusive government around. The government simply created an atmosphere of peace and prosperity for people to function in. That they dwelt under their own vine and fig tree also speaks to the whole issue of capitalism. Each person and family had the right and responsibility to create their own livelihood without overbearing government interference. *They understood that government's place was not to meet their needs, but rather to empower society and its people to meet their own needs.* If this were realized, government would stop trying to police, control, and be the answer to everything. It would put the power back in the hands of the people and be a source of empowerment rather than an intruder. Government is not supposed to be big. President Gerald Ford said, "A government big enough to give you everything you want is a government big enough to take from you everything you have."[3]

Israel's government by nature was a decentralized form of government leaving most of the decisions to be made in the city gates by the leaders of the city, not by the national powers. This caused a peace to be available and every man to live under his own vine and fig tree.

Even Paul in writing to Timothy exhorted that the church's purpose in praying for leaders in the civil arena was to have an atmosphere of peace to dwell in. First Timothy 2:1-2 shows this:

> *Therefore I exhort first of all that supplications, prayers, intercessions, and giving of thanks be made for all men, for kings and all who are in authority, that we may lead a quiet and peaceable life in all godliness and reverence.*

Through the prayers of the church, we can help create the right spiritual forces for kings to make the right decisions. This will allow people to live a quiet and peaceable life in godliness and reverence. When this is done, the atmosphere is created for the kingdom of God's increase. When the church does its job and the governmental leaders lead with righteousness and integrity, there is a peace established that causes all things to flourish.

The reformed government mountain also executes justice against workers of wickedness. Protection of society and its citizens is another function of proper government. One of the reasons for some of the chaos experienced in society is the lack of judgment toward wicked and evil acts. Ecclesiastes 8:11 tells us that evil works not being judged with enough severity actually encourages evil to be present within a society:

> *Because the sentence against an evil work is not executed speedily, therefore the heart of the sons of men is fully set in them to do evil.*

We see this in our society today. People worthy of great punishment and even the death sentence are allowed to linger for years without the ultimate punishment being rendered. This does nothing but encourage the *sons of men* to do evil. The government mountain is the place from which the judgments that need to be rendered are to flow. Many bleeding hearts in the government realm have promoted ideas that have led to evil being able to take root within our society rather than being eradicated through proper judgments. Romans 13:4 along with I Peter 2:14 show us that one of the purposes of authority and government is to punish and execute wrath against evil:

> *For he is God's minister to you for good. But if you do evil, be afraid; for he does not bear the sword in vain; for he is God's minister, an avenger to execute wrath on him who practices evil* (Romans 13:4).

*Or unto governors, as unto them that are sent by
him for the punishment of evildoers, and for the
praise of them that do well* (I Peter 2:14).

When evil is punished, it sets in place boundaries
that many are much more reluctant to cross. With
this in place, the greater part of society is free to live
in peace and enjoy a safety created by proper government being expressed.

As the sphere of government is reformed, there will
also be an applauding of that which is good. Just like
there should be a rendering of judgment against crimes
committed within society to protect society from the
onslaught of evil, there should also be a commending
of the good that is accomplished. Romans 13:3 says
that when we do good, the civil authorities are there to
commend and reward as well:

*For rulers are not a terror to good works, but to
evil. Do you want to be unafraid of the authority? Do what is good, and you will have praise
from the same.*

Rulers are to praise the good. One of the primary
examples of this is when Israel was dealing with Goliath
in the days of Saul. We are told that Saul had promised to reward whoever brought the giant down with
riches, his own daughter as wife, and his household

being freed from any taxes past or future. First Samuel 17:25 communicates this promise that was rehearsed in the ears of David:

> *So the men of Israel said, "Have you seen this man who has come up? Surely he has come up to defy Israel; and it shall be that the man who kills him the king will enrich with great riches, will give him his daughter, and give his father's house exemption from taxes in Israel."*

In this setting government and its rulers were willing to reward any citizen who was able to bring down the giant threatening the nation. It would be good for government to learn that you always get more of what you applaud. When we applaud the right stuff, we get people performing within society accordingly. When we reward either directly or indirectly wrong behavior, we get more of that. A reformed government will know how to reward right behavior with benefits that reflect that behavior and not reward behavior that does damage to society. For instance, the rewarding of welfare benefits to those who use the system for livelihood instead of becoming productive parts of society should be outlawed. Government has created this scenario that sucks millions and even billions of dollars a year into a black hole and does nothing but promote carelessness and irresponsible living. If government would commit itself to give tax breaks to those who create jobs and promote the economy and society, much good would be done instead. Instead, those who are doing this are punished with higher taxes rather than rewarded for their overall good effect on society. This would be a sure way to improve society and the morale of society as well.

As the government mountain is reformed, a willingness to acknowledge and listen to the prophetic voice of God will follow. In biblical times, the government mountain and the religion mountain were always linked together in Israel. We are not advocating a religious state, but we are advocating an influence of the prophetic into the lives of governmental leaders.

A great deception has been propagated concerning the issue of separation of church and state. This originated through a letter written by Thomas Jefferson. His purpose for advocating the separation of church and state was not to protect the state from the church but rather to protect the church from the state. In other words, he was not concerned about the church bearing influence on the governmental structure but rather the government seeking to restrict religious freedoms. This has been used to try and limit and annul the church having influence within the framework of government.

But within the reformed government mountain, there will be an invitation for the church and the prophetic to be involved with each other from their respective mountains. Second Kings 6:8-10 shows us this in operation and as a result, a nation and its armies are spared from ambush and defeat:

> *Now the king of Syria was making war against Israel; and he consulted with his servants, saying, "My camp will be in such and such a place." And the man of God sent to the king of Israel, saying, "Beware that you do not pass this place, for the Syrians are coming down there." Then the king of Israel sent someone to the place of which the man of God had told him. Thus he warned him, and he was watchful there, not just once or twice.*

It became a way of living for the king of Israel to listen to and even rely on the prophetic of his day. The prophetic is not there to rule the nation but to help with divine awareness for the leader of a nation. The decisions will still be left to the government mountain—it is just that the prophetic can bring a word that can help give direction to a nation and its leaders. How we desperately need leaders today who are open to divine input into their leadership as they seek to order nations in today's world.

Connected to this prophetic input into the government mountain, there will also be the joining together of *king* and *prophet* in prayer that will affect the heavens and bring answers in times of crisis. Something very special can happen when the government mountain joins with the prophetic from the religion mountain. Great solutions are released from heaven. We see this when Hezekiah the king joined with Isaiah the prophet to seek the Lord concerning the enemy that had risen to threaten the nation. Second Chronicles 32:20-21 records how God answered the prayer of the king and the prophet when they mixed together and created a spiritual synergy that resulted in the deliverance of a nation:

> *Now because of this King Hezekiah and the prophet Isaiah, the son of Amoz, prayed and cried out to heaven. Then the Lord sent an angel who cut down every mighty man of valor, leader, and captain in the camp of the king of Assyria. So he returned shamefaced to his own land. And when he had gone into the temple of his god, some of his own offspring struck him down with the sword there.*

The prayer of the king and the prophet not only released angelic help and delivered a nation from a military conflict, it also caused the one from whom the threat came to be eradicated. There is great power when the government mountain acknowledges the prophetic and allows it entrance into its sphere and function. Many enemies of our nation and the nations could be destroyed through the mixture of the prophetic into government issues. Again, I am not suggesting a religious state being created. It is just that when government and the religion mountain acknowledge each other and join together, clearly enemies that oppose society and nations are destroyed.

Another thought concerning the government mountain in a reformed state is that it produces an environment for evangelism. We do not expect for government to be party to the evangelism efforts of any group, but neither do we expect it to hinder them. Again, we are not advocating a religious state of any kind. But when government is in a reformed state, an atmosphere will be created that propels evangelism forward. First Timothy 2:1-4 tells us that as the church prays for its leaders an atmosphere of quietness and peace is produced that propels the purposes of evangelism:

> *Therefore I exhort first of all that supplications, prayers, intercessions, and giving of thanks be made for all men, for kings and all who are in authority, that we may lead a quiet and peaceable life in all godliness and reverence. For this is good and acceptable in the sight of God our*

Savior, who desires all men to be saved and to come to the knowledge of the truth.

When the church is exercising its God-given role in the life of the government mountain, there will be quietness and peace that allows the desire of God to see men saved be realized. This occurs because of the governmental authority of the church over the powers of the devil that want to influence the government mountain. When the church does its job, the unseen powers of darkness that want to manipulate government and oppress society as a result are broken. The result is the heavens being open over the government mountain and this sphere having the kingdom of God's influence in it. So when the government mountain has come under the authority of the kingdom of God, an order will come to society that will allow the claims of Jesus in the earth upon men's hearts to be fulfilled. Proper government always empowers religious expressions and never limits them.

Some would argue that we need limitations on some religious groups. My answer to that is only on those who are propagating crimes against people, children, and others in the supposed name of God. Other than that, the truth of the Gospel is more than powerful enough on a level playing field to sway the hearts of people and draw them to the Lord. When this is there through proper government, the purpose of the kingdom will be driven forward.

NOTES

1. Draper, *Draper's Book of Quotations,* 5196.
2. Ibid., 5198.
3. Ibid., 5168.

CHAPTER 12

THE REFORMED GOVERNMENT MOUNTAIN
Part 2: The Empowering Mountain

To see the mountain of government reformed there are four distinct strategies we should employ. First, we must recognize that principalities target government because of the power to influence all of society through this mountain. When the powers of darkness known as principalities can bring governmental officials into alignment with themselves, they can then orchestrate their diabolical intentions in the earth realm. This occurred during the reign of Herod when he put the apostle James to death, then sought to do the same to the apostle Peter. Through the prayers of the church, this scheme was dismantled. Acts 12:1-3 shows how the devil used this ruler to work this travesty against the kingdom of God in the earth:

> *Now about that time Herod the king stretched out*
> *his hand to harass some from the church. Then he*
> *killed James the brother of John with the sword.*
> *And because he saw that it pleased the Jews, he*
> *proceeded further to seize Peter also. Now it was*
> *during the Days of Unleavened Bread.*

Herod came into agreement with the principality so that this entity worked through the government mountain to resist the kingdom of God in the earth through the apostles. Again, because of the positioning of government in society and its ability to influence, it will be targeted by the powers of the devil. When we realize the battle we are in for the government and what is at stake, it will heighten our commitment to seeing this mountain reformed.

We must also operate as the ecclesia or governmental people of God and pray. Through the church or the ecclesia of God, we have the power to bring down the principalities and free government from their rule. Ecclesia is the Greek term that Jesus chose to use to describe His people of government in the earth. Matthew 16:18 says this church or ecclesia is what Jesus would build:

> *And I also say to you that you are Peter, and on*
> *this rock I will build My church, and the gates of*
> *Hades shall not prevail against it.*

The ecclesias of Jesus' day were the governmental people of cities or societies who made decisions that determined what their cities or societies looked like. The term ecclesia is a secular term and not a religious one. If we understand this, we realize that the government of God through His church can exercise influence over the natural governments of the earth through the spiritual realm and prayer. Of course, we do this through the Courts of Heaven. As the *ecclesia* we stand in the legal realm of the spirit and undo any claim being made against us. This allows God's will to be done in the earth rather than what satan desires.

This did happen in the book of Acts as the church or ecclesia prayed. In Acts 12:12 we find the governmental people of God exercising their authority in the house of Mary:

> *So, when he had considered this, he came to the house of Mary, the mother of John whose surname was Mark, where many were gathered together praying.*

Many were praying for the release of Peter. The word *many* means "sufficient or enough." So regardless of the number that was there, there were plenty in the spirit realm to accomplish the task. As a result of this expression of the ecclesia praying, an angel was sent to deliver Peter out of jail, and this same angel later smote

Herod because of the judgment against a corrupt governmental official who was impeding God's will in the earth. Acts 12:23 shows how the judgment of God was rendered and the government mountain was altered because of the prayer power of the ecclesia of God:

> *Then immediately an angel of the Lord struck him, because he did not give glory to God. And he was eaten by worms and died.*

God struck down and removed corruption from government because of the prayers of the church. We must know that as we pray, powers are broken, the heavens are rearranged, and the way is made for God's will to be done in the earth.

As we prepare to invade the government mountain, we must be committed to voting. The casting of our vote is not just letting our voice be heard, it is a statement of conviction in the spirit realm. Believers must be motivated to involve themselves in the political process if we are to reclaim the mountain of government. We must shake free from lethargy and take back what belongs to the kingdom of God. As part of Jesus' governmental people called the *ecclesia*, we are to legislate in the spirit through prayer, but then implement the victories we have won in the spirit into the natural. Among other things in the government realm, this means we need to vote. Voting is an enforcing of the victories we have warred for in the spirit.

Reclaiming the government mountain will involve preparing and placing reformers into governmental position. These reformers must come forth from the coming generations so that we can begin to infiltrate this mountain. It is impossible to pray well enough that we have no need for reformers with a kingdom agenda in their hearts. We must see these people who are called to the government mountain take their place at every level. This will produce a reformed mountain of government that will empower us. Matthew 13:33 speaks of the effects of the kingdom of God being like leaven. You hide it in meal and pretty soon the entire lump is leavened out:

> *Another parable He spoke to them: "The king-*
> *dom of heaven is like leaven, which a woman took*
> *and hid in three measures of meal till it was all*
> *leavened."*

If we can get the right reformers prepared and in place as leaven within the government mountain, we will see this mountain and all the others taken for the kingdom. If we can get the reformers in place, then the host of heaven and the Spirit of God will be able to work their agenda through these people instead of the powers of darkness. The reformation of this mountain requires a new breed of leaders who can implement the will of God in this realm. Producing reformers is one of the greatest challenges that we face. As we engage ourselves in this endeavor, we will see God's blessing on it—reformers placed and the mountain of government beginning to reflect the splendor of God's kingdom. This mountain will be a fashioning element into all of society as it is reformed and begins to take on the convictions of God in its function in the earth.

PRAYER POINTS
for the Courts of Heaven

1. Pray for our present governmental leaders to be led by the Lord.

2. Pray for a government that produces an atmosphere for peace, protection, and empowerment.

3. Pray against and bind every demonic force that wants to hinder God's purpose in the earth through our government officials.

4. Pray for a breed of new reformers to come forth with a passion to lay their lives down to change every corruption in government.

5. Pray for a government that empowers and does not intrude into the lives of families.

As we come before Your Courts, Lord, we pray for those in authority over us, that we might lead a quiet and peaceable life. We ask that the heart of these in governmental places would be turned by Your hand. We ask that every demonic power seeking to control them would be caused to cease and desist its influence over them. We ask for a judgment against these powers from Your Courts in Jesus' Name.

We ask, Lord, that our government would be that which produces peace, protection, and empowerment for us. Let the government of this nation be party to the peace of God ruling in our culture. Undo any spirit that would seek to bring upheaval. Allow Your peace instead to rule and reign among us. I also ask that Your protection might be upon our nation. Would You cause Your divine guardianship to be with us. Lord, set Your care over us as a people, we pray, and deliver us from all evil. Don't allow injury or harm to come to us, but protect us from the hatred of the devil. We also ask for the empowerment to prosper to come from our government. Would You cause each one of us to dwell under our own vine and fig tree without fear. Thank You for wisdom being granted to our leaders to produce an atmosphere that allows prosperity to come.

We also ask, Lord, that every governmental leader, on every level, would be under the influence of the heavenly realm and not the demonic. We request that a judgment would come from Your Courts to bind and make ineffective any and all demonic sway against our governmental leaders. Let them be touched and affected by You instead. Silence all wrong counsel before them that they might only hear the counsel of the Lord.

We also petition You, Lord, that a new breed of reformers would arise. Replace our system with those who would father a nation rather than political leaders. Give us rulers who desire Your heart for this nation and not to make themselves rich. We ask for a removal of leaders who are corrupt. Let them be displaced and allow righteousness to reign.

We ask, Lord, for a government that would lead in Your heart, but not intrude. Let there be a government that is truly of the people, for the people, and by the people. Bring reformation to our government that Your

kingdom will might be done in the earth. We
ask this for Your sake, in Jesus' Name, amen!

— 184 —

CHAPTER 13

THE REFORMED BUSINESS MOUNTAIN
Part 1: The Finance Mountain

Regardless of our station in life, everyone is influenced and touched by the business mountain. Whether we are in the business realm to make a living or simply as consumers, we are involved in the business mountain. When you look throughout scripture, you will find people often in both the business mountain and the religion mountain. Paul and his traveling companions, it seemed, quite often functioned in both. Paul even exhorted those who were a part of his team to employ themselves. Titus 3:14 shows us Paul exhorting those who were his co-laborers to be active and involved in the business arena of their day:

And let our people also learn to maintain good works, to meet urgent needs, that they may not be unfruitful.

Paul realized that operating in the business mountain while seeking to establish the kingdom of God in a region went hand in hand. This is why he spoke of this endeavor producing fruitfulness for the kingdom purpose. He also said it would meet the urgent needs of the ministry and of their own lives. So Paul saw the involvement of his team in the business mountain as a strategic part of establishing kingdom rule in a region. He also addresses this in I Thessalonians 4:11-12 by exhorting the Thessalonian Christians to keep honest and good employment and endeavors in the business mountain:

> *That you also aspire to lead a quiet life, to mind your own business, and to work with your own hands, as we commanded you, that you may walk properly toward those who are outside, and that you may lack nothing.*

Those who were a part of the business mountain while expanding the kingdom of God were to lead a quiet life, have their mind occupied with their own pursuits, walk in a righteous way toward those who were not believers, and have every need met and lack nothing. It is obvious that activity in the business mountain was a way of life for Paul and his ministry team. Paul himself was a tent maker who worked with his own hands so that he would not be a burden to budding churches and could dispel every accusation that he was *in it for the money*. Second Thessalonians 3:6-9 relates this idea:

> *But we command you, brethren, in the name of our Lord Jesus Christ, that you withdraw from every brother who walks disorderly and not according to the tradition which he received from us. For you yourselves know how you ought to follow us, for we were not disorderly among you; nor did we eat anyone's bread free of charge, but worked with labor and toil night and day, that we might not be a burden to any of you, not because we do not have authority, but to make ourselves an example of how you should follow us.*

Paul said that even though they could have exercised their authority as apostles, they chose to work in the business realm instead to create an example for others to follow.

Many men and women of God today are finding that God has indeed called them to both mountains. They are anointed for the religion mountain, but also for the business mountain as well. When we lose the idea that one is spiritual and the other is secular and realize that both are about service to God, we are free to operate this way. Not every person in the religion mountain will be anointed to function in the business mountain also, but some will. They must have the freedom and liberty to exercise themselves in both spheres without an old wineskin mentality that they should dedicate themselves to *ministry* only. This comes from the separation between spiritual and secular. There is no such separation in God. Everything is spiritual and should be approached as such before the Lord. The idea of the separation of secular and sacred has a demobilizing effect. This comes from the Greek mindset and not the Hebrew one. When I speak of a Hebrew mindset, I am speaking of the concepts that God had His people operate from. We are told in Psalm 24:1 that everything is sacred to the Lord.

> *The earth is the Lord's, and all its fullness,*
> *The world and those who dwell therein.*

The Lord claims all the earth, the world, and all its inhabitants as His. He rules over them and can use them for His divine purpose. Therefore, everything can be considered to be sacred. We must shake free from the mentality that one is more holy than the other. Then we can realize that God wants to use us in our function, whatever mountain we are called to.

There are several purposes for which God uses the business mountain. If we are to recognize it in a reformed state, we should first realize the worth of this mountain before the Lord. When we do, we will then be able to see how the mountain functions when it is reformed.

The business mountain is to be a channel through which we and our families obtain provision. Scripture says that God opens His hand and provides for every one of His living creatures. He satisfies the longing of every one. Yet each one must arise every day and go into the business realm and gather in what God is providing. Psalm 104:27-28 announces that God is the provider and we are those who must gather in what He is providing:

> *These all wait for You,*
> *That You may give them their food in due*
> *season.*
> *What You give them they gather in;*
> *You open Your hand, they are filled with good.*

This all occurs in the business mountain. Everyday people arise and go to work in the business dimension to gather in what the Lord is graciously providing. When we see it this way, we realize that God is the source of all things. This causes us to have a right perspective and dependence on Him.

The Lord also uses this mountain to finance the kingdom of God. It takes wealth to see the work of the kingdom accelerate. God will bless some extraordinarily so that they can propel the kingdom of God forward. We see this in Luke 8:1-3, where some women of means were able to substantially provide for Jesus, His team, and their work in the kingdom:

> *Now it came to pass, afterward, that He went through every city and village, preaching and bringing the glad tidings of the kingdom of God. And the twelve were with Him, and certain women who had been healed of evil spirits and infirmities — Mary called Magdalene, out of whom had come seven demons, and Joanna the wife of Chuza, Herod's steward, and Susanna, and many others who provided for Him from their substance.*

These women had been touched and changed by the ministry of Jesus. As a result, they gladly gave to support and empower His work in the earth. It became a love act and a thank you to the Lord to be able to sow into the ministry that God had granted Him. People who finance the kingdom with their wealth because they have been touched by the goodness of the Lord have no other motive or agenda than to love God and humbly help His purposes forward in the earth. They are not trying to control or buy favors, but rather to extend the kingdom rule with the wealth that God has entrusted them with. This is one of the main uses that flow from the business mountain.

God also uses this mountain to destroy poverty from the earth. It is the desire of the Lord to get such prosperity flowing in the earth from this mountain that systemic poverty, or systems that hold people in poverty, is dismantled and removed. It is possible that such blessing can flow out of this mountain that poverty ceases to be an issue in a society. I know this sounds crazy and too good to be true, but the Lord said it. Deuteronomy 15:1-5 tells us that some of the laws of God governing economics could be suspended because the blessing of God had come so strong that there were no poor among them:

> At the end of every seven years you shall grant
> a release of debts. And this is the form of the
> release: Every creditor who has lent anything to
> his neighbor shall release it; he shall not require it
> of his neighbor or his brother, because it is called
> the Lord's release. Of a foreigner you may require
> it; but you shall give up your claim to what is
> owed by your brother, except when there may be
> no poor among you; for the Lord will greatly bless
> you in the land which the Lord your God is giv-
> ing you to possess as an inheritance — only if you
> carefully obey the voice of the Lord your God, to

> *observe with care all these commandments which*
> *I command you today.*

When God's people carefully obeyed the voice of the Lord, poverty that had possessed some would be eradicated. Therefore, certain laws that God had set up to help the poor would no longer be needed. The blessing of God on the business mountain would cause all of society to be blessed and people to be experiencing the plenty of the Lord.

When Jesus came to earth, the first thing He said He was anointed to do was to deal with poverty among people. Luke 4:18 tells us that Jesus was anointed to preach the good news to the poor. The good news to the poor is that Jesus has come to remove their poverty and to cause them to prosper:

> *The Spirit of the Lord is upon Me,*
> *Because He has anointed Me*
> *To preach the gospel to the poor.*

The gospel of the kingdom has the power to break poverty out of a society and individual people when it is believed, adhered to, and obeyed. At the core, poverty is an individual issue. There are systems that can be dismantled that hold people in poverty. However, even without this happening, when individuals apply the principles of the kingdom to their lives, they will be made to prosper. God will guide, lead, speak to, bless, and empower a person to come out of poverty as they practice these principles. The Lord will bless these people in the business mountain and cause them to prosper. Psalm 128:1-2 tells us that God's blessing will be upon a person's work when they fear the Lord:

> *Blessed is every one who fears the Lord,*
> *Who walks in His ways.*
> *When you eat the labor of your hands,*
> *You shall be happy, and it shall be well with*
> *you.*

Eating the labor of the hands speaks of what a person's work has produced. It says that we will eat and be happy and things will be well with us because the blessing of the Lord has been secured as a result of our fear of Him. The fear of the Lord always equates to obedience and faithfulness to His word.

It is the blessing of the Lord on those who fear Him that can break the spirit of poverty and allow God's blessing to flow out of the business mountain and into lives and society. Deuteronomy 8:2-3 shows us when we obey Him that He teaches us how to hear His voice that leads us to prosperity:

> *And you shall remember that the Lord your*
> *God led you all the way these forty years in the*

wilderness, to humble you and test you, to know what was in your heart, whether you would keep His commandments or not. So He humbled you, allowed you to hunger, and fed you with manna which you did not know nor did your fathers know, that He might make you know that man shall not live by bread alone; but man lives by every word that proceeds from the mouth of the Lord.

God allowed a season of lack and of need so that they would not depend just on their conventional wisdom. They would also and more importantly listen for His voice. He very clearly says the whole purpose behind this process was to teach them that the proceeding word leads to provision. To break the spirit of poverty, we must obey and listen for the voice of the Lord. It will lead us to the place of provision if we take the time to be seasoned in the process. We will not live just by bread alone, but by every word proceeding from the mouth of the Lord.

As people function in the business mountain, we will also see this mountain reformed. Every day that people go to work, they should not just be going to earn a living, but to reform a mountain. This is what we must have if we are going to see reformation impact our society. There are some significant ideas that the apostle Paul laid down concerning life in the business world or marketplace. Ephesians 6:5-9 shows us from the slave and master relationship how we should relate as employees and employers in our day. I am not saying that when you work for someone that you are a slave. My point is that these principles Paul addresses can be applied to our working in a job that serves another person's agenda. As we live out these practical instructions, in a practical way we reform this mountain while earning our living:

> *Bondservants, be obedient to those who are your masters according to the flesh, with fear and trembling, in sincerity of heart, as to Christ; not with eyeservice, as men-pleasers, but as bondservants of Christ, doing the will of God from the heart, with goodwill doing service, as to the Lord, and not to men, knowing that whatever good anyone does, he will receive the same from the Lord, whether he is a slave or free.*
>
> *And you, masters, do the same things to them, giving up threatening, knowing that your own Master also is in heaven, and there is no partiality with Him.*

As employees serve their employers from the heart with a good attitude, they will not only earn a paycheck. They will reform a workplace and be rewarded by the

Lord Himself. We are told that we are to be *serving the Lord* as we do our job in the workplace. Not only will we earn our wage, but our attitude in the midst of our service will also allow the Lord Himself to reward us. Employers who treat their employees well and do not abuse, oppress, or insult them will also be rewarded by the Lord for the way they function in the workplace. If these simple things were done by those who occupy the business mountain every day, there would be a grassroots reformation that would occur. This can only happen as we stop just making a living and start reforming our sphere of society in this mountain.

Before we see what the business mountain looks like reformed, there is one final thing that God uses the business mountain for that I want to mention. The business mountain will provide, as Dennis Peacocke says, the "engine for reformation" into all the other mountains. We are not going to reform any mountain without the necessary finances to accomplish this. Great wealth will be required to see this endeavor done. The finances for the entire reformation effort will flow from the business mountain, which means that this mountain is the *financing mountain* in regard to its overall effect upon society. God will use this mountain in a reformed state to finance His kingdom's work in the earth. He will place such a blessing on people that they will become a conduit for kingdom wealth to flow. They will be a pipeline to finance the agenda of the Lord in the earth. The Lord will raise up entrepreneurs, corporations, and businesses that will produce great wealth for the sole sake of financing reformation. There must be this level of wealth created and released for this job to be done. Isaiah 60:5 promises us that the "sea" or the masses of humanity will come with wealth for the purposes of the kingdom:

> *Then you shall see and become radiant,*
> *And your heart shall swell with joy;*
> *Because the abundance of the sea shall be turned*
> *to you,*
> *The wealth of the Gentiles shall come to you.*

I realize this is a promise made to the Jewish people by God. However, because we have been grafted in, we have access to these words as well. The Gentiles or those who are unsaved shall come and bring their wealth. We must realize, when we speak of reforming society, that we can even partner with unsaved people who are good humanitarians to get God's agenda done in the earth. God will even use their finances for His will in the earth. We must take off unnecessary limitations we have placed on ourselves. We are to remember that the earth is the Lord's, and the world and all that dwells therein (see Psalm 24:1). As we mentioned earlier, God used a heathen king named

Cyrus to send His people back to Israel after the Babylonian captivity to rebuild the temple and the nation. He gave them wealth and provision to accomplish this task (see II Chronicles 36:22-23). He caused the Egyptians to give to the Israelites provisions of gold, silver, and fine things as they left Egypt. The Bible says they spoiled the Egyptians (see Exodus 12:36). It is possible for the Lord to take the wealth of the world that belongs to Him and grant it to His people through the business mountain to reform society.

Many of the founding fathers of America were wealthy people before the revolution began. They were so committed to the cause of the revolution that they spent all their wealth to finance the armies and the endeavors of establishing a new nation. There were many of these brave and heroic people who, though they had great wealth at one time, died penniless as a result of their commitment to the revolution. This brought reformation to the whole world. I am not saying that we should expect to die penniless. I am saying that it will take this same kind of commitment if we are to see a revolution that reclaims our society. There will be those whom God can trust with great amounts of wealth who will use it to see society reformed.

One of the reasons we must have the finances flowing from the business mountain is that wealth always creates authority. We see this in Matthew 25:20-21, where Jesus tells the parable of the master who entrusts his servants with varying measures of money. He then comes back to receive the increase from what they have gained:

> *So he who had received five talents came and brought five other talents, saying, "Lord, you delivered to me five talents; look, I have gained five more talents besides them." His lord said to him, "Well done, good and faithful servant; you were faithful over a few things, I will make you ruler over many things. Enter into the joy of your lord."*

Notice that the master did not reward those who had handled the money rightly with more money. He rewarded them with authority and rulership. Finances stewarded and used correctly will always lead to places of influence, authority, and rulership. Wealth and riches do grasp the attention of our society. Money does grant influence. When we have money, it equates to influence on a major level. People will listen, hear, and even heed because of the level of a person's wealth. Bill Gates has no problem getting an audience with anyone because he is a rich and wealthy man. As God finds those He can trust in the business mountain, He will promote them into great places of wealth, not just to finance reformation, but to hold places of authority and influence that others will respect. Their voice can and will be used to shape the mountains they are in.

CHAPTER 14

THE REFORMED BUSINESS MOUNTAIN
Part 2: The Finance Mountain

Let's look at the business mountain in a reformed state. Five distinct characteristics will be realized in this mountain as it comes to a reformed state. At the core of the reformed business mountain is an *honor for God*. As Nehemiah brought reformation to Jerusalem and the nation of Israel, he reestablished the Sabbath. No business dealings were to be done on the Sabbath. This day in Jewish law was set apart to honor the Lord. As Nehemiah rebuilt the city physically, he then re-inhabited it and began to put city life and its society back in place. In the book of Nehemiah, we see people treading grapes in wine presses, bringing in sheaves, loading donkeys with produce to bring into Jerusalem—all on the Sabbath. Nehemiah contended with the nobles because this was strictly forbidden for the Jewish people by the mandates of God. Their dishonor of this day was a dishonor of God. Nehemiah 13:17-18 tells us that he rehearsed in their ears how wrong this was and the consequences it could bring.

> *Then I contended with the nobles of Judah, and said to them, "What evil thing is this that you do, by which you profane the Sabbath day? Did not your fathers do thus, and did not our God bring all this disaster on us and on this city? Yet you bring added wrath on Israel by profaning the Sabbath."*

The greed of the people that propelled them to dishonor the Sabbath and therefore dishonor God had to be addressed. The business mountain of this nation had allowed its covetousness to press them past an honor, worship, and respect of the Lord. As they broke the Sabbath, they were dishonoring the God who had hallowed it.

I am not suggesting that we keep the Sabbath or even close our stores on Sunday, even though some of the most successful Christian businesses have chosen to do this in honor of God. Hobby Lobby and Chick-fil-A have been honored by God because they have honored the Lord and the day of worship normally acknowledged in our culture, which is Sunday. Their commitment to put God above the desire for a good profit margin has resulted in the blessing of the Lord coming on their businesses. All I am saying is that, however it is fleshed out, when the mountain of the Lord is reformed there will be tangible expressions of an honor of God above the making of money.

The reformed business mountain also has within it an honor for men. So often the workers who propel our economy forward are seen more as slaves than as people. When we look at scripture, we see a great honor being displayed between employers and employees. Ruth 2:4 shows us how Boaz, the owner of the field or business, related to his employees and how they related to him:

> *Now behold, Boaz came from Bethlehem, and said to the reapers, "The Lord be with you!" And they answered him, "The Lord bless you!"*

What a wonderful environment to work in and be a part of. Boaz obviously had a respect in his heart for those who worked for him, and the workers clearly had an affection for their boss. So often this is not seen in corporate America. The bottom line is not about the workers but about the work. Could it be if this kind of mutual honor was present that there would be much more productivity than what we have now? In a reformed business mountain, the people are more important than the product, creating a loyalty that would result in greater productivity.

I can hear some now thinking that if they created this kind of work environment nothing would ever get done because of the propensity of our work force to be slackers. They would take advantage of the kindness and not repay it with due diligence. My suggestion to that is fire them and get some people who will. I am not suggesting that we tolerate laziness and non-excellence. I am saying that we train a new breed of worker who responds to honor and therefore gives it back in loyalty, diligence, and productivity.

In I Timothy 6:1-2, Paul echoes these sentiments of a reformed business mountain:

> *Let as many bondservants as are under the yoke count their own masters worthy of all honor, so that the name of God and His doctrine may not be blasphemed. And those who have believing masters, let them not despise them because they are brethren, but rather serve them because those who are benefited are believers and beloved. Teach and exhort these things.*

Notice the honor that is to be shown in the workplace. The masters or employers are to be honored and served. Paul said these things were to be taught and exhorted. We can change and bring reformation if we teach people these principles. Otherwise, we are destined to continue to repeat the past or even something worse. As the mountain of business is reformed, honoring people will become a premium and even an affection shall be established. A loyalty will arise that will astound all who witness it. Mutual respect can go a long way in producing productivity in the work place. Where this kind of honor is given, an atmosphere of care and concern is nurtured. This could be a demonstration of heaven on earth in the marketplaces of nations.

In the reformed mountain of business, there is no oppression caused by greed. Greed is a sin that causes people to be oppressed. Out of a desire for increase and accumulation, people are not given their rightful lot and earnings. This is what the apostle James was alluding to in James 5:1-6:

> *Come now, you rich, weep and howl for your miseries that are coming upon you! Your riches are corrupted, and your garments are moth-eaten. Your gold and silver are corroded, and their corrosion will be a witness against you and will eat your flesh like fire. You have heaped up treasure in the last days. Indeed the wages of the laborers who mowed your fields, which you kept back by fraud, cry out; and the cries of the reapers have reached the ears of the Lord of Sabaoth. You have lived on the earth in pleasure and luxury; you*

have fattened your hearts as in a day of slaugh-
ter. You have condemned, you have murdered the
just; he does not resist you.

The rich held back the wages of those who worked for them and the cries of the oppressed had reached the ears of the Lord. When you read this scripture closely, you find that the wages held back *cry out* themselves. It appears the wages that rightfully belong to others, mixed with the cry of the laborers, causes judgment to come on oppression caused by greed. Remember that the Lord is the righteous Judge. When that which is unjust is brought before His Throne, He can and will judge it to be illegal and unrighteous. The result can be removal of those who have money and giving it to those who will handle it correctly. We should be those who make these cases in the Courts of Heaven against oppressive economic systems.

The Lord said that the rich had fattened their own hearts like an animal that was being made ready for slaughter. Greed is a very evil thing. It controls men's hearts and causes them to hurt and wound others. All of this is done to get wealth and make money. Paul spoke of greed when he spoke of the love of money in I Timothy 6:9-10:

But those who desire to be rich fall into temp-
tation and a snare, and into many foolish and

harmful lusts which drown men in destruction and perdition. For the love of money is a root of all kinds of evil, for which some have strayed from the faith in their greediness, and pierced themselves through with many sorrows.

People who give themselves over to greed end up with many sorrows in their hearts and even stray away from the Lord in their desire to be rich. There is nothing wrong with being rich as long as our hearts are not consumed in greed. The Lord will let us have money if money doesn't have us. In other words, I must not have covetousness, greed, or any other such thing in my heart.

The Lord actually set safeguards into place in Israel's economy to keep greed out of the economic system. The Year of Jubilee was one of these safeguards that kept greed from taking root. Every 50 years, everything went back to the original owner and family. Leviticus 25:13-17 shows us how the Year of Jubilee was used to keep people from oppressing each other through greed:

In this Year of Jubilee, each of you shall return to his possession. And if you sell anything to your neighbor or buy from your neighbor's hand, you shall not oppress one another. According to the number of years after the Jubilee you shall buy from your neighbor, and according to the number of years of crops he shall sell to you. According to the multitude of years you shall increase its price, and according to the fewer number of years you shall diminish its price; for he sells to you according to the number of the years of the crops. Therefore you shall not oppress one another, but you shall fear your God; for I am the Lord your God.

When a business transaction took place, consideration was always given to how long the people would get to use what they were purchasing until it went back to the original owner. This in and of itself caused greed not to take root in the fabric of society. Of course, I am not saying we should return to the years when these principles were lived by. However, I am saying that they reveal the tendency in man's heart toward greed. If we are to be reformers in the business mountain, we must guard our hearts from these grievous things taking root. As the mountain of business is reformed, there will be an expulsion of greed that causes so many problems within this mountain and society. The mountain of business will become a pure expression of the kingdom as greed is removed from it. We must pray, believe, and work for this mountain of business to be free from greed and its consequences. When this is true, greed will no longer drive the economy; rather, seeking the blessing of the Lord will. Proverbs 10:22 tells us that the blessing of the Lord makes rich. This will become the pursuit of people operating in the business realm and not the manipulation of people through the spirit of greed:

> *The blessing of the Lord makes one rich,*
> *And He adds no sorrow with it.*

Greed may lead to riches, but remember there is sorrow associated with it eventually. When the blessing of the Lord produces riches, there is no such sorrow. As greed is untangled from the business mountain, many practices will change. Perspectives will shift and the blessing of God will come as this spirit is rendered powerless and broken in its influence.

The blessing of the Lord for wealth flows out of honoring, worshiping, and remembering the Lord. Deuteronomy 8:18 tells us that the Lord blesses with the ability to accumulate wealth:

> *And you shall remember the Lord your God, for*
> *it is He who gives you power to get wealth, that*
> *He may establish His covenant which He swore*
> *to your fathers, as it is this day.*

The Lord is looking through the earth for places to place His wealth into the hands of those who will use it to establish His covenant purposes in the earth. He has and is taking many through the process of removing greed and covetousness from their hearts, so He can bless them in the business mountain and use them as His vessels to distribute wealth for social reformation.

As reformation arrives, there will also be a deep heart for the afflicted and needy. Out of the prosperity of the business mountain, a tremendous heart of compassion will flow. Again, in Israel's economy God ordered the laying aside of three distinct tithes. There was a tithe that went to the Levites every year. There was a tithe that went to the landowners themselves. In other words, they tithed to themselves. This was commanded by God and was a savings plan that was theirs for financial security. The third tithe was gathered every third year and it was for those who were in need. Deuteronomy 26:12 shows us that from each Jew's business there was tithing that met the needs of the socially deprived and needy.

> *When you have finished laying aside all the tithe of your increase in the third year – the year of tithing – and have given it to the Levite, the stranger, the fatherless, and the widow, so that they may eat within your gates and be filled.*

This mountain will minister abundantly to those who are in need in our society. Part of the reason for this is that the spirit of greed will have been broken and it will be the joy of the heart of businesses to do this. An overflowing heart to minister compassion to the needy and afflicted will come forth. This will be the spirit that drives the business mountain as it reflects the kingdom of God. Nehemiah 8:10 tells us how we should operate:

> *Then he said to them, "Go your way, eat the fat, drink the sweet, and send portions to those for whom nothing is prepared; for this day is holy to our Lord. Do not sorrow, for the joy of the Lord is your strength."*

Eating the fat and drinking the sweet speaks of the blessings and prosperity of the Lord. As Nehemiah was bringing reformation to society, this was his admonition to them. However, notice that in the midst of prosperity, they were to *send portions to those for whom nothing is prepared.* This says that those who were in need were not to be forgotten. The reformed business mountain will be used of God to help the unfortunate. They will be taken care of and empowered into a better life. As some have said, not just a momentary hand out, but a hand up into the future is what the Lord would have for them.

A closing idea concerning this mountain is that lifestyles that have been earned will be enjoyed. We should get to eat from what has been produced and enjoy it. This is at the very core of our capitalist society and way of doing business. We are a free-market system and this is from the Lord. God is a capitalist at His core. Many of the parables that Jesus spoke had a capitalist mentality about them. In Matthew 20, for example, Jesus spoke of a vineyard owner who went out and gathered laborers to work in his vineyard at different times during the day. He then paid them what they had agreed to work for or what they trusted him to give them. In verses 14 and 15, this owner answers those who complained about the way he paid those who worked for him:

> *Take what is yours and go your way. I wish to give to this last man the same as to you. Is it not lawful for me to do what I wish with my own things? Or is your eye evil because I am good?*

Notice that because this man worked in a capitalist or free market system, what he had produced was his. He could do with it whatever he wanted. God is not a socialist or a communist. He is a capitalist. In the parable of the talents, in Luke 19:24-26, the faithless man who had been given the one measure was dealt with harshly.

> *And he said to those who stood by, "Take the mina from him, and give it to him who has ten*

> *minas." (But they said to him, "Master, he has*
> *ten minas.") "For I say to you, that to everyone*
> *who has will be given; and from him who does*
> *not have, even what he has will be taken away*
> *from him."*

As a result of this man not bringing increase to his master's wealth, what he had was taken away and given to the one who already had the most. The other servants protested. They didn't think that the one who already had the most should get more. They were socialist in their mindsets. However, God is a capitalist. He will give His stuff to the one who has exhibited the greatest ability to bring increase to it. God is a good business man. If we want more from Him, we must use what we already have. As a result of this capitalist mindset, we can do what we feel is right with what we have been given and have earned. Whatever we produce we can do with as we want. This is why we are free to enjoy the lifestyle we have created through the blessing of God in the business mountain. First Timothy 6:17-19 says the same concerning us enjoying things:

> *Command those who are rich in this present*
> *age not to be haughty, nor to trust in uncertain*
> *riches but in the living God, who gives us richly*
> *all things to enjoy. Let them do good, that they*
> *be rich in good works, ready to give, willing to*

> *share, storing up for themselves a good founda-*
> *tion for the time to come, that they may lay hold*
> *on eternal life.*

When we obtain riches, we must be careful not to trust in them but rather keep our confidence in God. This is what the Lord warned Israel of as He led them into the Promised Land full of plenty. They were not to allow the abundance there to cause them to forget God (see Deuteronomy 8:10-11). We must also use our finances and any wealth we have to build a firm foundation for times to come through using our monies for kingdom purposes.

In the midst of all of this, we are also to enjoy the things that God has blessed us with. This is the whole issue of the reformed mountain of business. As we function in this mountain and secure the blessing of God over our lives, it is proper for us to be rewarded with the lifestyle we have earned. This is a free market and capitalism at work. People's hard work, ingenuity, skill, favor, education, and blessing are to be rewarded in the business mountain.

As we go forth to reclaim and reform the business mountain, may it reflect the glory of God's kingdom. Through this mountain, the money and wealth necessary to reform all of society will be released. The business mountain is the *financing mountain* of society.

May the power of God be upon us and the strategies of the Lord be unveiled for us as we go forward in reforming this important mountain of the Lord.

PRAYER POINTS
for the Courts of Heaven

1. Pray for a revelation of the business mountain as the financing mountain for reformation of society.

2. Pray for the arising of entrepreneurs who create corporations for kingdom wealth for reformation purposes.

3. Pray for the spirit of greed that possesses the present business mountain to be destroyed.

4. Pray for creative ideas to be released for the birthing of wealth.

5. Pray for reformers of great influence to arise to lead corporations in the business mountain.

As I come before Your Courts, Lord, I petition You for the reformation of the business mountain. May those who function in the mountain, as called of You, recognize You would use them to finance Your kingdom purpose in the earth. Let them see that this mountain is the finance mountain for reformation of society and culture.

Lord, as I stand in Your Courts, I would also ask that there would arise entrepreneurs who carry the anointing of God for wealth. Would You raise these into places of prominence and influence. Let them be divinely set by You so that the wealth produced can finance Your will in the earth. Lord, we ask that Your desire would never be frustrated because of lack of funding.

We also ask, Lord, that the spirit of greed that has controlled this mountain would be judged as illegal and unrighteous. This spirit of greed is keeping the wealth needed for Your purposes locked up. May this thing be judged before Your Courts and found out. May it be brought to justice as a fugitive from the law right now in Jesus' Name.

We also request before Your Courts that there would be a birthing of wealth through Your people. Grant creative ideas, inventions, favors, and supernatural understanding. From these, Lord, cause that which makes rich and adds no sorrow to it to come into the hands of the righteous for kingdom dispersal in Jesus' Name.

I ask as well, Lord, that there would arise those to lead major corporations in the nations. Let men and women with kingdom hearts take their place in these decision-making places. Let the wealth of these corporations be used for Your agenda in the earth. We request that this might be set in place from the Courts of Heaven in Jesus' Name, amen.

CHAPTER 15

THE REFORMED ARTS AND ENTERTAINMENT MOUNTAIN
Part 1: The Prophetic Mountain

A rts and entertainment is a very powerful force within societies. From this mountain, there is a great influence that is released that can shape the look and nature of societies and their cultures. Arts and entertainment within our culture definitely has a voice. It is a prophetic voice to our culture. Hence the arts and entertainment mountain is the *prophetic mountain*. This means that what flows out of this mountain fashions, forms, and creates what society believes and stands for. We know this is true, because we see in Hebrews 11:3 that God formed the worlds through the word of His mouth.

> *By faith we understand that the worlds were framed by the word of God, so that the things which are seen were not made of things which are visible.*

When we look in Genesis 1:1-3, we see that the Lord spoke the "word" under the movement of the Holy Spirit.

> *In the beginning God created the heavens and the earth. The earth was without form, and void; and darkness was on the face of the deep. And the Spirit of God was hovering over the face of the waters. Then God said, "Let there be light"; and there was light.*

The result was the formation of the earth and its order. This is what the prophetic word does. Released long enough and consistent enough, it will fashion the way we think and operate. This is what those who function in the arts and entertainment arena understand. I like to say, "They are not entertaining, they are educating." They are espousing their belief system and values through the venue of their expression. They are actually prophesying to a culture. This is used to change, alter, and arrange the mindset of our society.

When Mary and our children were young and in school, we would take Friday afternoon as an opportunity to go to the movies. This was the one time we could have by ourselves before the children got out of school for the weekend. Sometimes it was difficult to find a movie good enough or morally sound enough that we wanted to subject ourselves to it. However, it was "our time" together in those very busy years. I remember one movie we went to called *In and Out* with Kevin Kline. We thought it seemed harmless enough. However, the movie was about a teacher who *comes out* as gay and how well he became accepted. This was not the first time this subject had been approached, but it was early on in seeking to get culture to accept the gay agenda. As we left the movie that day I thought, *We weren't just entertained, they sought to educate us.* We were being *prophesied* to that the gay lifestyle is normal, loving, and should be accepted as such. I began to realize that arts and entertainment was a prophetic tool to fashion the way a culture thought. This is absolutely true. We must retake this venue and mountain. We are seeing strides in this, but must continue to go after this all important realm of influence in society and culture.

On another date, we decided again to go to see a movie and again picked one from a less than stellar group of choices. This one turned out to be about nothing but teenagers having sex. Through this venue they were shaping the minds of a generation. They were not just saying that it was okay to have sex as a teenager, but that there is something wrong with you if you aren't having sex in your teenage years. Through the arts and entertainment mountain, a whole generation was being prophesied to and shaped by the voice coming from the movie screen.

In a reformed state, this mountain will have several benchmarks. We will get to several, but allow me to continue my thoughts with regard to this mountain's prophetic power. When I speak of a prophetic voice, again, I am talking of that which shapes society. Like no other mountain, this is what the mountain of arts and entertainment is. John 1:23 tells us John the Baptist's response when he was asked who he was:

> He said: "I am 'The voice of one crying in the wilderness: "Make straight the way of the Lord,"' as the prophet Isaiah said."

When the scripture speaks of *making straight the way of the Lord*, it is speaking of reformation. In other words, something has become perverted and crooked and God has come to straighten it out. This is accomplished through a *voice*. Reformation always begins with a voice—a prophetic voice. As a prophetic sound is released into a society and culture, that society and culture eventually begins to be shaped by the sound going into it. This is what happened in the days of John the Baptist. His prophetic voice prepared and straightened things out for Jesus to come into the earth. John's prophetic voice caused the society of that day to begin to be shaped into a state of reformation. Through the creative, prophetic release from the arts and entertainment mountain, the prophetic voice of God can begin to impact a culture.

Whatever sound and voice comes out of this mountain, society becomes and embraces. Through television, music, art, theatre, films, sports, and all the other venues, a prophetic sound is trumpeted into society. We must have those who are called, gifted, and creative in this mountain to send forth a sound that people within our society will run to.

God has always used this mountain to prophesy to nations and societies. The devil knows this and has again sought to hijack this venue away from us so he can sound his voice through this medium. During the War of 1812, as Fort McHenry in Baltimore was being defended from a vicious onslaught of the enemy, Francis Scott Key arose after a night of ferocious battle to find that the American flag was still waving over the fort and it had not fallen into the enemy's hand. As he gazed at this still waving flag, he penned the poem that later became "The Star-Spangled Banner," the anthem of our nation. This song has stirred the courage and stamina of many throughout the years. It has been a prophetic declaration of the fearlessness of the American people to fight even when all seemed lost. This standard came out of the arts and entertainment mountain. It is a prophetic sound as sure as any other that has been used by the Lord to rally the heart of a people in a land born by God.

Following the September 11th attacks of 2001, many songs from varying artists were birthed. Whether they were country, pop, secular, or religious, these songs motivated a nation and spoke to the heart of a trembling people. These songs, these words put bravery and resolve into a people whose faith could have wavered and even fainted. God again used the arts and entertainment mountain to prophesy power and might back into the heart of the people of the nation of America. This is just another example of the prophetic nature of this mountain flowing out of the creative juices of the Lord. This mountain at its core is a prophetic voice that must be harnessed to impact our society and shape it for the purposes of God.

As this mountain comes to a reformed state, it also serves as an echo. The prophetic essence of this mountain *shapes* while the echo nature of this mountain *reveals and reflects* what we as a society have become. The things we allow, pay to see, applaud, and support from the arts and entertainment mountain say volumes about the value system of a society. Like no other mountain, the arts and entertainment mountain is a revelation of where we are as a nation. If we want to see where the decency level of a people is, we only need to look into this mountain, which will give us a glimpse into the true nature of any people and can pro-vide us with prayer agendas that need to be focused for our society to be reformed.

Another important role this mountain plays is the refreshing of the soul of man. Perhaps due to its pro-phetic nature, there is refreshing that comes from this mountain into society and individuals as a whole. Psalm 23:3 shows us that it is God's heart to refresh the soul of people:

> *He restores my soul;*
> *He leads me in the paths of righteousness*
> *For His name's sake.*

The restoring of the soul is essential to life. If our souls are not restored, we will eventually lose heart, faint, and even die. There is recreation or a "re-creat-ing" of our beings that flows out of this mountain. This is why sporting events are such major attractions in our society. Some would say it is an *escape* from *real* life for a few hours. This may be true, but it is really the restoring of the soul that is taking place. All of us need this or we will become warped in our thinking and less than effective in our jobs, pursuits, and endeavors.

Psalm 78:57 speaks of a *deceitful bow* and people who are like this symbol:

> *But turned back and acted unfaithfully like their*
> *fathers;*
> *They were turned aside like a deceitful bow.*

A deceitful bow is one that doesn't shoot straight. The arrow may be good and accurate, but the bow will not let it hit the target because it has become warped. No matter the skill of the archer, the crooked bow will cause the arrow to go astray. The bows used during biblical times would become deceitful or crooked if they were never unstrung because the wood would begin to warp.

We are the bows God uses to shoot His purposes, plans, and destinies at the targets that the Lord has established. We can become warped and deceitful because we are never unstrung. This speaks of our soul needing to be restored and our being recreated. Some people do not realize this and therefore never allow themselves the privilege and pleasure of this process.

God made us spirit, soul, and body. We take care of our spirit through communion with the Father. We take care of our body through nutrition, rest, and exercise. We also have to take care of our soul, and part of this is the refreshing that flows from the arts and entertainment mountain. Oral Roberts — the great minister known around the world for his healing ministry, for evangelism, and for the educator he became — is reported to have relaxed through the reading of western novels. This was ministry to his soul. He recognized that just like his spirit needed to be built up and his body needed nutrition, so his soul needed the inspiration that came from the arts and entertainment mountain. When we realize this, we begin to see how important this mountain is not just to society, but to us as individuals as well. Without it we become very dull and boring and will eventually experience the law of diminished returns because our soul is famished and not in a restored state. What we could be accomplishing in life and destiny will be stunted because we haven't learned to refresh our souls.

The arts and entertainment mountain is designed to inspire the soul of man as well. The Lord uses the prophetic nature of this mountain to stir the fires and passions of ordinary people to attempt to do extraordinary things. From this mountain there is an infusion of courage that rallies the weak and fearful heart to believe and achieve the impossible. How we need this impetus in our lives and societies.

I am a sports fan, and sports movies have always arrested me in my soul. Some would think it is about sports, but it really isn't. It is about the underdog winning when it seems absolutely unreachable or unattainable. Several years ago, a movie came out about a young man in the 1970s who wanted to play football for Notre Dame. The problem was he was too small and slow. Even when they told him there wasn't a chance, he wouldn't give up or quit. He *won* himself a spot on the practice squad that was never allowed to suit up for games. He spent his entire eligibility working and waiting for one chance to take the field for the *fighting Irish* on Saturday afternoon. Just when he was promised that the following year he would be given the opportunity to suit up for at least one game, the coach left and another one who didn't know the young man came on the scene. This coach had no history with the young man and saw him only as a practice squad player.

The movie climaxes with the players taking matters into their own hands and demanding that this young man get the opportunity to suit up for his last opportunity and game as a senior. He finds himself on the sidelines but with seemingly no chance to enter the game. If you have seen the movie *Rudy,* you know what happens. The whole stadium eventually begins to chant, "Rudy, Rudy, Rudy." The pressure mounts on the coach as the assistant coaches, players, and the whole stadium begin to exert pressure for Rudy to play.

Finally, the coach relents, sends Rudy in, and the dream of an underdog is reached and fulfilled because he wouldn't quit or give up. The team picks Rudy up and carries him off the field as the movie ends. This expression from the arts and entertainment arena has birthed courage, drive, inspiration, and endurance for many because of the prophetic spirit released that inspires the soul.

We must have this unction released through these venues if we are going to see society impacted. We need people who have had their dying hearts revived and caused to live again as a result of the arts and entertainment world prophesying into and inspiring their soul.

As this mountain comes to a reformed state, it will also magnify the beauty of the Lord into all of society. Psalm 27:4 speaks of the beholding of the beauty of the Lord Himself:

> *One thing I have desired of the Lord,*
> *That will I seek:*
> *That I may dwell in the house of the Lord*
> *All the days of my life,*
> *To behold the beauty of the Lord,*
> *And to inquire in His temple.*

The beauty of the Lord is displayed in many different ways. All of His creation declares His glory and His splendor (see Psalm 19:1-4). As the creativity of the Lord is released through the arts and entertainment mountain, we will see various descriptions of His beauty that are breathtaking. As this mountain prophesies from a reformed state, God will unveil His character and nature for all to see. He will disclose aspects of Himself that impact the heart and soul of man even when they don't know they are encountering God. He will show pieces of Himself that touch and minister to the very depths of man's being. It could be through a sense of awe at a painting, song, theatric production, or any number of other displays. It could be through tears as presentations reach deep into the heart of a person and touch a heretofore untouched place of the soul. It could be through humor until deep wounds and hurts are healed in the experience of laughter. As prophetic unctions are heralded from this mountain, people will encounter the presence and power of the Lord, whether it is considered secular or spiritual. The Lord pays no attention to these labels. He will not be boxed in. He will send forth His prophetic message through this venue as His creativity is ushered into society through this mountain.

Carrie Underwood's song "Jesus, Take the Wheel" was a tremendous hit on the Billboard charts. Even though it spoke of Jesus, it wasn't considered a religious or spiritual song, but a country song. The song is about a young woman who almost has a terrible accident with her small child in the car. The incident parallels her personal life that is falling to pieces, and she needs someone to save her. She cries out, "Jesus, take the wheel" of my car, but more importantly of my life. This song probably caused more people to cry out to Jesus in the desperation of their lives than all the preachers presently preaching. God used this song to declare His saving power and grace if people would just cry out and reach toward Him. This is the power of the arts and entertainment world and the display of the beauty of His grace and kindness toward us.

This mountain will also recognize in a reformed state that its creativity flows from the Lord and His presence. Psalm 87:5-7 speaks of the place from which creativity on the level that I have been discussing flows. It flows from the very fountains of the Lord and His presence in and through our lives:

And of Zion it will be said,
"This one and that one were born in her;
And the Most High Himself shall establish her."
The Lord will record,
When He registers the peoples:
"This one was born there." Selah
Both the singers and the players on instruments say,
"All my springs are in you."

Zion that is spoken of here was a place in the Old Testament where God chose to dwell. It was the habitation of His manifest presence (see Psalm 132:13-14). It was the hill outside the walls of Jerusalem where David set up a place of worship, and God's presence invaded and filled that place always. The Old Testament Zion was a place, but the New Testament Zion is a people. God doesn't inhabit places now; He inhabits a people who belong to Him and are filled with the worship He loves. Psalm 87:7 says:

> *Both the singers and the players on instruments say, "All my springs are in you."*

When the Bible speaks of springs it is speaking of the creative juices of God flowing in us and through us. In the place and people of His presence, the creativity of a supernatural God is free to operate in that people.

Remember that God's agenda is to touch the earth and not just the people inside a church building. Isn't it interesting that so many Motown artists of the '60s and '70s came out of the church? They came out because the music that was in them and that they sang was deemed inappropriate for the church. Yet much of their music was about relationships and the struggles in them. Some were filled with inappropriate ideas of sexual immorality, but many were just echoing the struggles of people within love relationships, and some were espousing the beauty of being in love. Yet because it wasn't *spiritual*, there was no room made for these expressions and the artists were forced into the *world* to do their music. Many ended up in tragedy and personal trauma because the temptations of the world became more than they could endure and they fell into the effects of sin. Could much of this have been averted if the church had made room for differing ideas and been able to embrace the diversity that flows out of God's heart? Could these artists have been stewarded differently? There was a clear spring of creativity in them that should have been recognized. Why must we draw such cold, hard lines and boundaries and force people to make choices when we could be more inclusive while touching the earth through their gifts and creativity?

CHAPTER 16

THE REFORMED ARTS AND ENTERTAINMENT MOUNTAIN
Part 2: The Prophetic Mountain

There is much that God wants to release into the earth through arts and entertainment. But for this to happen, the church that stewards the presence of the Lord must allow that same presence to unlock creativity in people and allow it to flow without putting the labels of secular or spiritual on it. If we can ever get past these barriers in our thinking, we might see God do something through the creativity of His people that will astound the world. All the creative springs of God are in His presence.

In Exodus 31:1-6, we see God choosing Bezalel, Aholiab, and those with them to take the plans Moses received on the mountain. Through their gifted abilities as artisans, they actually built the tabernacle as a place for God to live among His people:

Then the Lord spoke to Moses, saying: "See, I have called by name Bezalel the son of Uri, the son of Hur, of the tribe of Judah. And I have filled him with the Spirit of God, in wisdom, in understanding, in knowledge, and in all manner of workmanship, to design artistic works, to work in gold, in silver, in bronze, in cutting jewels for setting, in carving wood, and to work in all manner of workmanship. And I, indeed I, have appointed with him Aholiab the son of Ahisamach, of the tribe of Dan; and I have put wisdom in the hearts of all the gifted artisans, that they may make all that I have commanded you."

One of the purposes that God will use the arts and entertainment mountain for is to build a place for His Presence to live. The Lord doesn't want to just dwell in what we call the church. He wants to manifest Himself in society as a whole. This can be accomplished through the creative release in the arts and entertainment mountain. God uses creativity as a means of expressing Himself in the earth. Creativity is at the heart of the arts and entertainment mountain.

In a reformed state, God will use this mountain to express and reveal Himself into the earth. This does not mean that everything will have to be religious or flow out of the church. Remember, we are to be a kingdom people, not just Christian. If we can grasp this in regard to the arts and entertainment mountain, we can see God's agenda pushed forward. I am referring to the beauty and splendor of the Lord being unveiled through many different dimensions of His creative nature. Hermann Cohen said, "Creativity is the basic attribute of God, identical with his uniqueness."[1] If this is true, then wherever God-inspired creativity is, God can be seen and known. My passion is to see a greater platform from which God can be known other than just within what we call the church. Even Solomon said that the house he had built for God could not contain God. First Kings 8:27 shows that even the splendor and greatness of the temple that Solomon built for God could not contain and house Him:

> *But will God indeed dwell on the earth? Behold, heaven and the heaven of heavens cannot contain You. How much less this temple which I have built!*

Solomon declared that not only the temple that had been erected, but the expanse of heaven was too small as well.

We must get God into society in every capacity. One of the chief ways is through the creativity that flows from the arts and entertainment mountain.

Hermann Cohen said that God's creativity helps establish His uniqueness. Our creativity helps establish our uniqueness and individuality as well. When the creativity of God is flowing through us, it separates us from others and helps set our own identity and even self-worth. Dorothy May Day expressed this idea even further when she said, "God is our Creator. God made us in his image and likeness. Therefore we are creators…The joy of creativeness should be ours."[2]

Creativity is that which causes life not to be mundane and lifeless. Without creativity, life becomes boring and fruitless. When we are being creative, we are being like God and experiencing His life flowing in us. This is the basic driving force of the arts and entertainment mountain.

The problem is that we have allowed this mountain to be hijacked. The church has either directly taught or allowed to be believed that all of this arts and entertainment stuff was *of the world* – and we were supposed to be separate from the world. As a result of this basic philosophy, we developed a hands-off mentality, and the devil came rushing into the vacuum created and took this mountain over. How ignorant and unlearned of us to think that the Creator of all the earth would not want us involved in creativity in the world He made. Just like all the other mountains, our neglect gave the devil opportunity to take over what God always desired and demanded for Himself. While we were making plans to *fly away* to heaven in a supposed rapture, the devil was entrenching himself in what is really the Lord's. We have some real repenting to do and then some real reestablishing to do as we seek to take back what the devil really didn't take but instead we gave away.

As we get ready to take back the arts and entertainment mountain, we should know at least partially what it involves. We are referring to theatre and fine arts, dance, television, music, artisans, film, and sports. These venues and perhaps others make up the arts and entertainment mountain that greatly impact and touch society. We must develop a new mindset in the church about arts and entertainment and not think of it as inherently evil or wicked. It is designed of God to influence on a grand scale when it is in a reformed state. Therefore, we should first see the church develop a new attitude about the creativity of God in its midst and then let it flow out into society. A kingdom mindset must be embraced.

As I was teaching on the arts and entertainment mountain, a young man came to me afterward. I had spoken that everything didn't have to be Christian but should instead be kingdom. This meant that we didn't have to make Christian movies or just sing Christian songs. We could and should instead make movies, songs, and other expressions that espoused a kingdom philosophy. Remember, these are the morals, ethics, values, and virtues of our King. As I completed my teaching, this young man came up to me. He began to declare that he had come to great liberty during this session. He was in fact a movie-maker and had been struggling with what kind of movies he should make. Should he make *Christian* movies or *secular* movies? Now he understood this was a wrong question. He knew now he was to make kingdom movies to prophesy to a culture and society of the King's heart.

As we completed our conversation, this young man turned to leave. I said to him as he walked away, "Thanks so much for sharing with me. You made my day."

He turned in response to me and said, "You made my life." Wow! I was stunned. This young man was now free from religious constraints to have a kingdom impact in culture. This is what the Lord desires.

We must see our young people turned loose with what God has placed in them without putting religious restraints on them. They are called of God to speak to a society through this tremendously important mountain. As the people of God are freed to function in the creativity of the Lord that is within them, society will be touched and changed.

There is much that God wants to release into the earth through arts and entertainment. But for this to happen, the church that stewards the presence of the Lord must allow that same presence to unlock creativity in people and allow it to flow without putting the labels of secular or spiritual on it. If we can ever get past these barriers in our thinking, we might see God do something through the creativity of His people that will astound the world. All the creative springs of God are in His presence.

As we finish up this chapter, let me give some ideas of how we may invade this sphere and see the creativity of God impact it and prophesy through it. If we are to impact this arena, we must get people free from captivity that is squelching creativity. Psalm 137:1-4 shows us how captivity of the soul stops creativity from flowing:

> *By the rivers of Babylon,*
> *There we sat down, yea, we wept*
> *When we remembered Zion.*
> *We hung our harps*
> *Upon the willows in the midst of it.*
> *For there those who carried us away captive*
> *asked of us a song,*
> *And those who plundered us requested mirth,*
> *Saying, "Sing us one of the songs of Zion!"*
> *How shall we sing the Lord's song*
> *In a foreign land?*

When Israel was taken captive into the land of Babylon, those who were there asked them to sing one of the songs of Zion. Their answer was that they were unable to sing one of these creative and life-giving songs as long as they were held in captivity. This is still true today. Many folks do not experience the creative power of God that is within them because their spirits and souls are bound in some captivity. Either from wounds, hurts, bitterness, sin, unwillingness to forgive, and other issues of the heart, they find the creative flow of God stopped and halted. There is an even greater hindrance and captivity, though, that is hampering the creativeness of God's people—the spirit of religion and the legalisms associated with it. The oppressive spirit of religion and legalism saps and destroys the creative juices of God. We must break the spirit of legalism that is holding the people of God captive and putting limitations on what is allowed.

We mustn't be so afraid of sin that we paralyze ourselves and others. I don't what to go into it all here, but the Holy Spirit must be granted the liberty to bring us into liberty so that we aren't living by rules and regulations but out of relationship with Him. When this occurs, God will dismantle many of the religious concepts that hold us and bring us into liberty to enjoy life. We see this in the life of Jonathan, the son of Saul, the first king of Israel. In I Samuel 14:27-29, we see

Jonathan eating some honey from the ground while a battle was raging against the Philistines. Saul had commanded the army not to eat anything before the setting of the sun so that God would supposedly honor them with victory. The problem was that Jonathan did not hear the command so he was *free* to eat:

> *But Jonathan had not heard his father charge the people with the oath; therefore he stretched out the end of the rod that was in his hand and dipped it in a honeycomb, and put his hand to his mouth; and his countenance brightened. Then one of the people said, "Your father strictly charged the people with an oath, saying, 'Cursed is the man who eats food this day.'" And the people were faint.*
>
> *But Jonathan said, "My father has troubled the land. Look now, how my countenance has brightened because I tasted a little of this honey."*

Jonathan was not under the oath that had been demanded or the legalistic requirement of his father, so he ate the honey and the honeycomb and his eyes and countenance brightened. This is what happens when we get free from the domination leveled at us by men. Our countenance and eyes brighten and the creative life of God begins to move in and through us. We must get the church free from this spirit of domination and legalism so that creativity may return.

In the process of invading the mountain of arts and entertainment, we will uncover and discover the gifts of God in us and among us. There are many gifts in the people of God that have not been allowed to function or at least have not been appreciated. If we can create an atmosphere where people and what they carry are honored and esteemed, we can see a prophetic impact enter the earth through this sphere.

Max McLean's remarks on creativity are perceptive and profound:

> Creative men and women are in the church. Some express their art through music, the only art fully accepted by the church. But others sit quietly alone; waiting to be affirmed, encouraged, supported. They are waiting for the body of Christ to understand and find room for the novel, the film, the play, the masterpiece ruminating within that could reach beyond the subculture and challenge the basic assumptions of our secular age and point the world toward ultimate truth.[3]

What a powerful statement about the true nature among God's people. We must make room and not just tolerate what is in people, but celebrate it. When will we move past just music and begin to develop novels, films, plays, masterpieces, and other forms to impregnate His people? When we do, we will move as a people from a subculture into a counterculture that is impacting life on the planet. The church has primarily been a subculture that is buried in the normal culture of society. No one really pays a lot of attention to it. This is terrible because we have become irrelevant. Nothing is worse than irrelevance. What we are to be instead is a counterculture. A counterculture is that which challenges the culture of society and changes it. We can only do this by entering the mountain of arts and entertainment and taking back the prophetic voice it carries. Through the medium of this mountain, we can shape a nation and society.

In order to really invade this mountain, we must get out of a church-only mindset and be brave enough to shoot for the mainstream of society. So often we have thought that we would win the world and reform society through what we did for a few hours a week in a building. How foolish of us. We must be free and empowered to take what is in us and attempt to go into mainstream with it. Remember, we don't have to preach at people—we can take these venues and through entertainment enter their lives with an anointing and wholesomeness that changes them forever. To do this can seem like a dangerous thing when we have been accustomed to living and functioning in the confines of a group of people called the church. But this will never change the world.

Oscar Wilde insightfully challenges us to think outside our comfort zones: "An idea that isn't dangerous is hardly worth calling an idea at all. It's the shock part, the frightening part, the unknown element that makes an idea an idea in the first place. If you feel comfortable with it from the very first, take another look. It's probably not an idea."[4]

We must be risk takers to be able to reform society. We must risk failure, rejection, humiliation, and any other thing that would try and thwart our attempts at changing society. Maybe they won't applaud our ideas. Maybe they will reject them. Or maybe we will be received. Maybe our ideas will be so novel that they find an audience and impress people of all groups. We will never know unless we risk it. If it seems dangerous, it could be an idea from God.

Oswald Chambers brings more insight into what can kill originality and creativeness: "Overmuch organization in Christian work is always in danger of killing God-born originality; it keeps us conservative, makes our hands feeble."[5] Thinking too much about a God-born idea can suck the very life out of it. We need to be as wise as we can, but never let the excitement and adventure be subdued by naysayers who say it won't work or can't be done. The world belongs to the risk takers, not those who play it safe. We must take the chance and go for it when we believe there is something innate in us from God for the world.

The last thought that I will mention about invading this mountain of arts and entertainment is that the hurts of life can become some of the greatest points that produce creativity. All of us have faced and experienced these places. There is something about the pain of life that can unlock new depths of creativity.

Marcel Proust said, in regard to this, that pain, injury, and struggle can lead to the beauty of the Lord being displayed: "We enjoy lovely music, beautiful paintings, a thousand intellectual delicacies, but we have no idea of their cost to those who invented them, in sleepless nights, tears, spasmodic laughter, rashes, asthmas, epilepsies, and the fear of death."[6]

Years ago as I was praying and listening to a new recording from a not-too-known group called Hillsong, I heard a song called "Shout to the Lord." As it played, I turned to one of my staff members and told them that we needed to learn that song because of the anointing on it. His response was, "Really." He didn't sense or feel what I felt. Sure enough, that song went on not only to impact the church but the world as well. It was actually performed on *American Idol* as a special done by all the remaining contestants at that stage. Who would have thought that a song from an unknown group would years later be known around the world and touch thousands upon thousands and even millions of people.

What most people don't know is the story behind that song and the one who wrote it and first sang it, Darlene Zschech. It seems that she was seeking peace from the Lord in turbulent times. From her book *Shout to the Lord,* she tells this brief story.

> It just happened to come out of my personal worship time with the Lord. Desperate for His peace, I opened to the Psalms. I sat at our old out-of-tune piano tinkling the keys, and "Shout to the Lord" flowed out from my heart. I sang it over and over again and it lifted me up. Over the next few days, the song stayed with me, and it began to dawn on me that it might be a worship song.

She was desperate for His peace. This troubling in her heart opened her spirit to this song that has touched millions. Knowing the background of that song places new power and might on it. It wasn't a little ditty written in an office or studio somewhere. It was a broken soul crying out in expensive worship to the Lord with a message that resonated to an entire culture. People may not know why the song ministers to them, but it is because of the anointing on it as a result of the expression of a broken heart to the Master.

There is great creativity in all of us. Pain embraced in God can actually unlock it and let it flow. Let all of us steward His creative nature in us, but especially those called to the mountain of arts and entertainment. We could just prophesy to a whole society and see it shaped for Jesus and His kingdom. The arts and entertainment mountain is the *prophetic mountain* of society that shapes society itself.

NOTES

1. Draper, *Draper's Book of Quotations,* 1999.
2. Ibid., 2002.
3. Ibid., 1998.
4. Ibid., 2013.
5. Ibid., 2014.
6. Ibid., 2021.

PRAYER POINTS
for the Courts of Heaven

1. Pray that the arts and entertainment mountain will be revealed as the prophetic mountain.

2. Pray for creativity to be unlocked out of the wisdom of the Lord to impact society.

3. Pray for finances to be unlocked to enter this prophetic mountain of arts and entertainment on a grand scale. We must hit the mainstream.

4. Pray for performers, entertainers, producers, screenwriters, songswriters, and other forms of artisans to arise as reformers and *prophets* in the arts and entertainment mountain.

5. Pray that a shift from Christian to kingdom will happen in God's people.

As we approach Your Courts, Lord Jesus, we thank You that You hear our petitions and requests. We ask, Lord, that we as Your people would recognize the arts and entertainment mountain as the prophetic mountain. Place within our hearts, we pray, a passion to release Your heart to our societies and cultures. We repent for giving away this venue to the devil. We ask that we might be empowered to reclaim it that Your word could go forth in and from this prophetic mountain. In Jesus' Name and for Jesus' sake.

We also petition Your Courts for the release of prophetic creativity. Unlock the souls of Your people from bondage of all kinds. Let Your wisdom and creativity flow through us to touch our generations. Free us from the spirit of religion and open our hearts to Your creative flow in Jesus' Name.

We also pray and request before Your Courts that finances will be released to produce and create that which will speak to cultures and societies on a cultural level. We ask for the enlargement of our dwelling places. Allow us, Lord, the privilege to affect the masses through these venues. May Your favor come that causes finances to be provided to fund Your word going to the masses though the arts and entertainment mountain, in Jesus' Name.

We pray, Lord, for performers, producers, directors, writers, entertainers, and all forms of artisans to be raised and set in place. Free these to express with creativity all that You have placed in them. Let them be liberated from all restraints and constraints to express the deepest realms of Your creativity, in Jesus' Name

Finally, Lord, as we stand in Your Courts, I ask that there would be the necessary shift from Christian mindset to a kingdom one. Let all religious training that has boxed people in from the kingdom agenda of God be removed in Jesus' Name. Let a new form of thinking take hold of our lives. Allow a kingdom expression of Your morals, ethics, values, and virtues to flow through this prophetic mountain of arts and entertainment, in Jesus' Name, amen!

CHAPTER 17

THE REFORMED MEDIA MOUNTAIN
Part 1: The Watchman Mountain

The media mountain is the mountain from which we get news of current events to discover their expected effect upon our lives and society. From this mountain, there is an attempt to shape the concepts and belief systems of a society. All we have to do is look at the reporting of the news and the information being given to see that there is an outright agenda. The mainstream media slants people's perceptions away from God and toward humanistic ideas. In the past few years, we have seen a phrase arise. There is such a mistrust of the news media that it is now referred to as *fake news*. This is a term to declare that what is reported as fact cannot be trusted or believed. The sad reality is, this is true. The media makes up stories, reports anything that would further their agenda, and ignores anything that would stand against it. Many people no longer have any confidence in the operation of the media of our day.

This is the main reason why we must retake this mountain of media. This will enable it to become a vehicle for the Lord to have His effect into society. We cannot deny the power and strength of the media on society. Therefore, if we are to reform society we must have this medium working on our behalf. This will require that we break the spiritual dominion presently influencing this mountain. We can then see reformers invade this sphere of society and its influence. Media is intended to inform and announce to culture any needed information. The media mountain is therefore the *watchman mountain*. It is set in society in such a way that it is to herald information. This allows society and the public to make decisions that concern them individually and as a nation.

The definition for *media* is "the main means of mass communication" (especially television, radio, newspaper, and internet). It implies all of these venues collectively as well. In a broader sense, the different expressions of media are news outlets, radio, internet, journalism, marketing, public speaking, and technology. As the *media* by definition means *mass communication,* clearly we see that this mountain has the power to sway the masses of humanity. This is what makes media so powerful, influential, and even dangerous when used wrongly. Media has been used by the enemies of the gospel and the kingdom of God to capture the hearts of people and make them believe wrong things. It has successfully in many situations done what the Bible warns about. It has turned light into darkness and darkness into light. In Isaiah 5:20, the prophet warns of this phenomenon as people become wise in their own eyes:

> *Woe to those who call evil good, and good evil;*
> *Who put darkness for light, and light for darkness;*
> *Who put bitter for sweet, and sweet for bitter!*

The media of our day has progressively taken certain ideas, and through their slanted reporting has made the information come to the masses in the way they desire it to be seen and heard. This is evil called good, good called evil. This is darkness for light and light for darkness. This is bitter for sweet and sweet for bitter. This is normally called *spin*. Spin is a normal part of the daily reporting of the news. As I alluded to earlier, however, it has become even worse than *spin* and is now *fake* and many times outright lies. Because these news agencies control the airways they are able to convince the masses of whatever they desire, quite often through their liberal and anti-God agendas and their attack on conservative values and causes.

The definition of *spin* is "giving a news story a particular interpretation." So the media doesn't just report the news today — they interpret it. The masses are told what they should think and believe about what was said, heard, or seen. Not through the reporting but the spinning of the news, they create a *thinking* throughout society. This thinking is in line with what they want the masses to believe and embrace. The first part of Proverbs 23:7 tells us how powerful the thinking of a single person is and therefore how powerful the thinking of the combined masses is:

For as he thinks in his heart, so is he.

However we think, that is what we become. Our thinking eventually determines what we act like, look like, and become. When the whole of the population's thinking is altered by the way the news is communicated, that is spin and even fake news. The spin put on it, to interpret and not just report the news, is a very strong attempt to change and cause people to adopt a way of thinking. This causes them to become that way in their minds and hearts. Add to this the celebrity of being on television, radio, the internet, and other forms of high-profile attractions. This causes people to be prone to believe wholeheartedly what is being said and communicated by and through that personality.

This is a deadly mixture and recipe for the swaying of society and culture.

The problem is the swaying is toward a decidedly anti-God agenda and an anti-Christ mentality permeating through the masses. The media is used by those who control it to a large degree to actually disciple nations and make them believe what they desire them to believe. Jesus said that we were called to disciple nations. As we have seen, Matthew 28:19 shows Jesus commissioning His apostles to disciple not just people but nations as a whole:

> *Go therefore and make disciples of all the nations,*
> *baptizing them in the name of the Father and of*
> *the Son and of the Holy Spirit.*

Instead of the church discipling nations, we have allowed the liberal agenda to disciple and fashion their thinking. They have taken over what God said was to be His. We must arise and take back this mountain so that we can change the thinking of a society and disciple nations as the Lord has desired.

The other mountains that we have discussed have varying effects upon society and its cultures. Some empower while others provide; still others equip and some shape values. The media mountain more than anything fashions the mindset of a society and a nation. As the watchman mountain, it has the responsibility to warn, alert, and inform without spin or fake news. Spin perverts the function and godly effect of this mountain. Through the constant barrage of spun news reporting, people began to believe lies instead of the truth. Truth begins to fall in the streets because of the belief system created from the media mountain into a nation. Isaiah 59:14-15 speaks of truth failing and justice being ignored. It also says that it greatly displeased the Lord:

> *Justice is turned back,*
> *And righteousness stands afar off;*
> *For truth is fallen in the street,*
> *And equity cannot enter.*
> *So truth fails,*
> *And he who departs from evil makes himself a*
> *prey.*
> *Then the Lord saw it, and it displeased Him*
> *That there was no justice.*

This is speaking of a society that has so forsaken the Lord and His ways that there is no justice, no equity, and no righteousness. This is so catastrophic that whoever repents and turns from evil becomes the enemy of that society and system. This can only occur when the mindset of a people has become so warped that it believes wrong things and embraces ungodly, immoral, and antichrist philosophies. The media is one of the main instruments that is used to accomplish the purpose and goal of liberals in any and every nation.

In the early days of the developing media that reported the news over radio and then television, the reporters were very careful to *only* report. They did not put their own ideas into their disclosures. I remember as a kid watching Walter Cronkite on the evening news. He was a great reporter who shared happenings around the world with the masses in America. In my recollection, I never remember there being a spin put on the news so that people would begin to believe what those in control wanted them to believe. There was too much nobility and honor for the position of reporting the news. This line was not crossed. Only in later years did it become known that Walter Cronkite had a very strong liberal leaning. Yet it was never known in those days, because he was careful to not abuse his place in society. He understood and lived by a creed that would not allow him the privilege of seeking to impart his own ideas or opinions to the American people. He was there to simply report the news and leave the interpretation of it to the people who were receiving it.

How so very different it is today. I can remember and see in just my lifetime how the news media has shifted. Whereas the early journalists were very careful to maintain that which they were trusted with, journalists of today are blatant concerning their own ideas and political concepts. Often, with clear disdain for anything that is Christian, godly, upright, and moral, they project their own philosophies daily into their reporting. They seek to progressively disciple a nation with their godless rhetoric and immoral mind-sets. We must have a shift back to the former days. The days when the media was a welcomed asset into society. It was not a poison that was bent on perverting everything away from virtue and God's cause in the earth. We must reclaim this mountain for the sake of society and the kingdom of God.

CHAPTER 18

THE REFORMED
MEDIA MOUNTAIN
Part 2: The Watchman Mountain

If we are to reform media with all the other mountains, we need to recognize what it will look like in a reformed state. As I rehearse these things that the media mountain potentially looks like in a reformed state, I will continue to reiterate the nobility that must exist within this mountain. There is such power within this mountain to influence the masses that it must be handled very carefully. Otherwise, harm will flow from this mountain rather than the good that God would use it for as the watchman mountain.

As this mountain is reformed, it will become a watchman on the wall for society. Watchmen were those who sat upon the wall of a city. They looked to make sure that nothing dangerous or harmful was coming toward the city. If there was something coming toward the city, then a trumpet blast was sounded. This warned and started the people toward a prepared state. This should be one of the primary functions of the media in society when it is in a reformed state. Whether it is getting information out concerning impending disaster or exposing harmful behavior or simply a warning concerning large parts of society being taken advantage of, the media should sound the trumpet as watchmen on the wall. Song of Solomon 5:7 shows one of the functions of watchmen:

> *The watchmen who went about the city found me.*
> *They struck me, they wounded me;*
> *The keepers of the walls*
> *Took my veil away from me.*

These watchmen struck, wounded, and took away the veil that was being hidden behind. This is what watchmen do in their effort to protect society.

For instance, weather warnings that come from the media mountain are invaluable. They protect and preempt many deaths on a yearly basis. Because of the warnings concerning hurricanes, tornadoes, and other weather related concerns, lives are saved. Also, the information that comes after disasters is essential in getting relief to the proper locations and in a timely manner. Without media outlets, these things would be much slower in occurring, if they ever occurred at all. The veils that these disasters would have hidden behind are taken away by the watchmen who have charge of the wall and city.

In contrast, these media outlets cannot become politicized. If they do, then they are used by a political bent to further their cause. This has been true of the COVID pandemic. COVID has been very serious. However, the news media has been used by political agendas to create confusion. Most people don't know what to believe or trust about the disease, vaccines, or what they should do. This is because of the history of fake news and spin. The media mountain has lost a measure of its credibility and therefore voice. There is such skepticism because of the hidden agendas of the news outlets that have been clearly exposed.

The media also has the right and responsibility to uncover corrupt political issues that wound and hurt society as a whole and the people in it. When hypocritical leaders are discovered, they should be uncovered so that they are held accountable by the people who granted them their office or position. This must be done without political partisanship. The media should and must be a politically neutral entity if it is to do its job as a watchman in society. Political agendas within the media have led to the need for this mountain to be reformed. If we can purge this mountain of political ambition, then the media would return to a pure state of reporting the news without interpreting it. It would then be a watchman on the wall for society and its concerns.

Sham artists and people who seek to take advantage of society—the unfortunate, the elderly, or just the uniformed—should also be exposed on a grand scale by the media arm in society. The ability to get word out concerning con men who are using the media themselves and in particular the internet should be uncovered. Their gig should be disrupted and stopped.

For this to occur within the media mountain, a right mindset must be in place. If the media is to be the present-day watchman, then it must be able to blow the trumpet from a right perspective. If a wrong belief in wrong philosophies is in place, they will sound an alarm against the wrong things. This is what happens often today. First Corinthians 14:8 speaks to us concerning trumpets that are giving a wrong sound:

> *For if the trumpet makes an uncertain sound,*
> *who will prepare for battle?*

If the trumpets being sounded in the media are giving an unsure sound, then people will not know how to respond accordingly. What we have at times in the media is the sounding of an alarm when there is no need for one. In the Old Testament, the priest would blow certain sounds on two silver trumpets. Certain sounds signaled the whole of the people to either gather together, advance, or be warned of issues that needed to be prepared for (see Numbers 10:2-7). They didn't make a certain sound for war when all they needed to do was release a sound to gather together. If they had, the people would have lost confidence in the trumpets. They would not have responded as they needed to. The trumpets were only sounded when they were needed in legitimate times of distress.

In current times, the media has fallen prey to being fear mongers rather than true watchmen. They have subtly and sometimes in an outright endeavor sought to use fear to get what they desired. They have painted pictures of certain candidates that have caused people to fear the election of them, when in fact it was a ploy to stop the masses from voting for them for political reasons on the media's part. It is not limited to politics. Even though it is politically connected, the media is guilty of seeking to create fear in regard to health issues. COVID and its variants are being promoted as a death sentence unless vaccines are taken. The problem is the vaccines are uncertain and leave much to be desired. Yet they endeavor to use fear to press the masses into their control. This is caused by the embracing of a wrong belief system that needs to change

IMPACTING THE SEVEN MOUNTAINS *from the* COURTS OF HEAVEN

within the media. There must be an invasion of a new breed of journalist who carries a right belief system and agenda so that there can be a clear and clarion call that is trumpeted from the media mountain.

The reforming of the media mountain will also involve the gathering and dispensing of information. Even though the media is to be a watchman on the wall, they must also realize that their job is to inform and leave the ultimate decision to those who hear the information. This has not been the mode of operation in our current state of affairs. The media is not content to just bring information; they want to also interpret it. Again, this is considered spin and even fake news. They must give the public the honor of and the privilege to discern the information. First Peter 2:17 exhorts us to show honor to all people. Honor is a basic human need. Everyone wants to be honored, valued, and esteemed:

> *Honor all people. Love the brotherhood. Fear God. Honor the king.*

Today, it is common for the media to steal away from the public their right to make up their own minds. The media's attitude is that the public is not intelligent enough to make the right choices. We need to be told not just information but what we should do with it as well. They tend to have an exalted view of themselves, as though they are the only ones who are smart. They must communicate to us lesser beings the choices we should make. What a dishonoring attitude that drives the present expression of the media.

For the media to be reformed, there must be a return to a simple communication of the facts and not an effort to interpret them. The honor of interpretation belongs to the people of a society, and it is not the right of the media to steal that away.

As the media mountain is reformed, there will be a purging of prejudice from this sphere of influence. First Timothy 5:21 lets it be known that prejudice and partiality are not allowed in the economy of God:

> *I charge you before God and the Lord Jesus Christ and the elect angels that you observe these things without prejudice, doing nothing with partiality.*

We are told that nothing is to be done with prejudice or partiality. Prejudice is an attitude against something or someone for biased reasons. Partiality is an attitude for someone or something for the same reasons. In the media, these two things must be removed. What this says is that the media cannot press its own agendas or desires on society. Their position of power and influence doesn't allow this. This is a misuse of that place of influence. If someone takes the position they have been given for public service and uses it to get their own agendas in place, that person or group has just disqualified and made themselves unworthy of the position they hold through prejudice and partiality.

Positions of power and influence must be stewarded appropriately. One should never use their place to dominate the whole from the perspective of the few. This so often happens through the media. The liberal and godless media is out of touch with the mainstream of America. Yet they use their place to manipulate things to where they desire them to be. The few overwhelm the real core values and belief systems of the greater whole with prejudice and partiality.

From prejudice and partiality, the media begins to fashion society and a nation in its thinking. To reform this mountain, those driven by their own agendas must be replaced by those who will honor the place they occupy with a nobility that it deserves.

This brings me to the next role that the reformed mountain of media will operate in. It will use its influence very carefully. In II Corinthians 10:8, the apostle Paul spoke of the right use of authority and influence:

> For even if I should boast somewhat more about our authority, which the Lord gave us for edification and not for your destruction, I shall not be ashamed.

Paul said that authority and influence were for edification and not destruction. In other words, authority is a very powerful thing and must be used with all wisdom and counsel. The media mountain must be filled with people of character and full of integrity who will use their position to serve the people of a nation. Jesus said that he who would be greatest must become the servant of all (see Mark 10:44). This is the only mindset and posture that qualifies us to occupy the place of great influence. Without the servant's mentality to serve others' needs and not our own agenda, we end up being tyrants rather than treasures to society. When the servant's heart is again within the media mountain, it will become a great blessing to the nation and not a self-serving icon that people cannot trust. The weight of its influence will increase exponentially as it takes on the heart that God desires. This will allow the Lord to pour Himself through it to influence nations and their societies.

The reformed mountain of media will also have a deep commitment to truth. Without truth being reported in a truthful way, things are being built on a faulty foundation. They will crater and fall. Right now in the news media, everything is relative when it comes to truth. Truth is whatever someone wants it to be. There are no moral absolutes. If a lie will get you want you want, then that is truth. This is the prevailing philosophy of our society. This is what Pilate implied as Jesus stood before him in John 18:37-38:

> *Pilate therefore said to Him, "Are You a king then?" Jesus answered, "You say rightly that I am a king. For this cause I was born, and for this cause I have come into the world, that I should bear witness to the truth. Everyone who is of the truth hears My voice."*
>
> *Pilate said to Him, "What is truth?" And when he had said this, he went out again to the Jews, and said to them, "I find no fault in Him at all."*

When Pilate said, "What is truth?" he was questioning what was really real and implying that there were no absolutes. When there are no absolutes then there is no integrity by which the game is played. The rules are changing constantly as a result of this.

If the media mountain is to be reformed, there must be a deep commitment to the truth. Otherwise, there is no confidence that the people can have. The trumpet sound coming from this watchman mountain will not be respected. When something is reported, it must be from a sincere heart leaving out no part of the truth out. Truth cannot be twisted to mean what someone wants it to mean. This is what happens and it is appalling to the Lord. Lying is such an abomination to the Lord that those who find themselves in eternal torment will have been guilty of it. Revelation 21:8 specifies liars as those who will be eternally judged.

> *But the cowardly, unbelieving, abominable, murderers, sexually immoral, sorcerers, idolaters, and all liars shall have their part in the lake which burns with fire and brimstone, which is the second death.*

So much of the national conscience has been formed by the lies of the media. We must take this media mountain back with a commitment to truth — Not half-truths that make it sound the way the liberals want. Not untruths that pervert so that people believe the wrong things. Only the whole truth that allows people to make right choices and decisions.

For this, we must produce reformers and journalists who will give a sound that people can run to. It is possible for us to reform this very important mountain. Let us rise up and build until the job is complete. Let us believe the mountain of media will become the watchman in society that blesses the public from a servant's heart.

PRAYER POINTS
for the Courts of Heaven

1. Pray for the influence of the media mountain as the watchman mountain.

2. Pray for an integrity and nobility to return to the media mountain and the removal of the liberal agendas and opinions.

3. Pray against the spin, fake news, and interpretation of the news rather than a simple reporting of it.

4. Pray for a clear sound to come from this mountain as a trumpet of the Lord.

5. Pray for a new breed of journalists to arise with the right sound who act as reformers in this watchman mountain of media.

As we approach Your Courts, Lord, we bring the media mountain to You. This mountain is set by You to be a watchman in society. I ask, Lord, that from this place there would be a right influence that would come into society and culture. Let every wrong, antichrist agenda in this mountain be judged and removed by Your Courts, I pray, in Jesus' Name.

I also request, Lord, that a great nobility would be returned to this mountain and the people who function in it. Let every godless and liberal agenda be exposed and removed. Allow the judgment of the Lord to come against any and all who would use this position to promote agendas against You, in Jesus' Name.

I also ask, Lord, that there would be a judgment from Your Courts against all spin, fake news, and outright lies being propagated through the media mountain. Allow that only a simple reporting would be done. Let the public be given the honor and respect to make their own decisions based on information given truthfully, in Jesus' Name.

I petition these Courts also, Lord, that from this mountain there would be a clear trumpet sound. Allow all fearmongering to be revoked. Let only a true sound of information and facts come before the public from this mountain of media, in Jesus' Name.

I also ask that there would be a new breed of journalist that would arise to take their place in the media mountain. I ask that people with right and noble hearts would be promoted into places of influence in this mountain. May they be reformers prepared by You to take their place. Let Your Courts render decisions that set these judgments in place, I pray in Jesus' Name, amen.

CHAPTER 19

THE SEVEN MOUNTAINS:
Social Functions

I have thought to finish this book many different ways. More than anything, I want it to be known that I realize that this is not an exhaustive account of what the mountains look like in a reformed state. There are many brilliant people who probably have a greater contribution than I do to this whole procedure of reformation. I simply responded to the word of the Lord to develop and write this book on what each mountain looks like in a reformed state. I knew I had heard the Lord when He spoke to me. My problem was I didn't have any awareness of what these mountains looked like in their individual reformed state. As I stepped into the word that I had heard, as is the case with any word from the Lord, there was a grace attached to it. I was amazed at the revelation that began to come to me from a prophetic viewpoint about the mountains in the reformed state.

My prayer and hope is that, if nothing else, this book stimulates dialogue and therefore true strategies to begin the reformation of each one of these mountains. Until we can begin that, all we have is concepts that may excite, but no real tactics to see reformation begin to occur. It is my hope and privilege to be one of the voices that God would use to begin this process and hopefully hand it off to the reformers of the coming generations to get the job done. As my friend Dutch Sheets has said, "Awakening in our day and Reformation in our lifetime."

As you can see, each mountain is discussed concerning its reformed state. As these ideas came into view, I began to recognize that each mountain had a very significant part to develop and release into the whole of society. I have *defined* each mountain with a descriptive subtitle that I think declares the core essence of what that mountain is in society. I would like to close this book by reiterating the importance of these mountains from the label I have attached them.

I have labeled the religion mountain the *impetus mountain*. This is because reformation will come forth from the church that is a part of this religion mountain. The church is to be the driving force behind the reformation of society. It is the church that will proclaim the need for reformation, create faith for reformation, and hopefully design some of the strategies for reformation into the nations. It will be a voice designed by God to stir people to believe change can occur. Jesus commissioned His first apostles and disciples to go forth and disciple nations. This is the reformation of society, and it flows from the mountain of religion that contains and houses the church. In my estimation, there will be no reformation in our lifetime unless the church is the impetus and driving force behind it. This requires that the church be reformed itself from a pastoral mentality to an apostolic entity that operates from a servant's posture. As this occurs, it will drive the reformation forward with inspiration, vision, and passion. From the religion or *impetus mountain*, a sense of divine destiny will enter many reformers' hearts, realizing they were created to impact society as they enter their mountain of calling.

The next mountain is the mountain of family. The family mountain is the *values mountain*. Out of this mountain, the value system of a nation comes forth. Without values, there is no foundation on which a society can build. In this sense, the family mountain provides a prophetic voice that stands for the standards of the Lord. Psalm 11:3 asked a rhetorical question, as we have seen, concerning the foundations of life.

If the foundations are destroyed,
What can the righteous do?

The fact is that there has been an eroding of family values in the nation for many decades now. When these values are washed away, the very fabric of society is changed. As the family and its core values are restored, they will flow into society and cultures will be reformed and reclaimed. The basic sense of decency, morality, ethics, honor, and many other noble attributes will once again govern and rule our world. All of these begin and flow out of the family mountain and into society as a whole.

The education mountain is the *equipping mountain*. Please remember that the religion mountain, the family mountain, and the education mountain create a pipeline for reformers to be produced for all of the mountains, which is necessary for the reformation of society. We cannot have reformation without reformers. Reformers have to be produced — and the impetus of the religion mountain, the values of the family mountain, and the equipping of the education mountain are all necessary pieces to the reformers being developed and sent into their God-ordained spheres.

Equipping is essential because it puts the intellectual and logical skills that are required into the hands of the people of society. It teaches budding reformers how to *speak the language* of their mountain of calling. Education is one of the best weapons against the enemy of poverty. When people are educated without an anti-God bias, education becomes a very powerful thing. The ability to read and to have printed materials during the Reformation of Martin Luther (that birthed the Protestant movement that resulted in much of the advances we have seen) granted education to the common man. This equipping propelled the Reformation forward, whereas without it, it would probably have never gained traction. Our young people must go into the education mountain to be equipped so they learn not just facts, but how to think and logic so they can have an answer that is intelligent within our world. Without the ability to reason and debate on an intellectual level, the impetus of the church will never produce reformation. This necessitates the educational process that flows from the education mountain without sapping the spirituality and love for God that our young people carry. When this is in place, they will be equipped to be reformers to their generation.

The government mountain is the *empowering mountain*. This is the proper purpose of government. So many people think it is government's responsibility to meet their needs. This is a welfare mentality that has possessed much of society. Government's purpose is to empower its citizens to meet their own needs. It isn't to intrude or invade the privacy of the citizens of a given country, but rather to provide the opportunities for people to make their own livings for their families. This has made America great up until this point. People have come from all over the world to plug into the American Dream. The idea has been that if you are motivated enough, smart enough, energetic enough, and wise enough you can build a life for yourself and your family in the nation of America. This has not always been true in other nations, but it was here at home. We have not been socialists or communists, but capitalists who knew if we produced, we could eat from it and the government would not interfere. In fact, government sought to help these things become a reality. This requires smaller government and not larger.

Government only gets big when it believes its purpose is to meet the needs of its citizens. This inherently leads to government domination of its people. But when government's purpose is to empower people to meet their own needs, then government is allowed to be smaller, less restrictive, and unobtrusive. This frees the individual and family to operate in the liberty of producing and eating from what they produce without government seeking to control and even take the lion's share of their wealth. Government should empower, not imprison.

The business mountain is the *finance mountain* of society. From the mountain of business, the reformation will be financed and paid for. Again as Dennis

Peacocke says, "Finances are the engine that drives reformation." As this mountain is reclaimed, it will finance the work of reformation in the earth. This requires that the right people control the funds. The Lord said in Deuteronomy 8:18 that He would give His covenant people the power to bring forth wealth:

> *And you shall remember the Lord your God, for it is He who gives you power to get wealth, that He may establish His covenant which He swore to your fathers, as it is this day.*

God wants His people to get wealth so His covenant purposes can be fulfilled and accomplished in the earth. This means that for God to do in the earth and in society what He desires, He must have a wealthy people to do it through. So we must have this mountain of business reformed and reclaimed so that it begins to reflect the splendor of the kingdom of God, but it also produces and releases the finances that will be the engine that drives reformation in the other six mountains as well.

The arts and entertainment mountain is the *prophetic mountain*. From the voice and sound sent out by this mountain, nations and their societies will be shaped. Voices always shape what they impact. Through the different expressions resonating from this mountain, people will become what is being prophesied to them and about them. For this reason, we must again possess this mountain that we neglected and turned over to the powers of darkness. As we recover it, there will be a sound coming from this mountain that will shape societies and disciple nations from its voice.

The media mountain is the *watchman mountain*. Through news outlets and everything else connected to this mountain, watchmen will arise who can make a clear trumpet sound without hidden agendas and spin placed on stories and reports. They will be used to uncover, disclose, warn, encourage, and impart necessary information so the public can make choices and decisions without pressure being exerted to feel a certain way about a certain thing. There will be a purity of journalism restored to this mountain and therefore a clear trumpet call made when necessary. The media will be that which the public can believe again without having to weigh everything through a suspicious filter wondering what is really being said and done.

These seven mountains—the religion/impetus mountain, the family/values mountain, the education/equipping mountain, the government/empowering mountain, the business/finance mountain, the arts and entertainment/prophetic mountain, and the media/watchman mountain—must be targeted with reformation in mind. We must begin to have a vision that we can run with for each one. We must have a prayer strategy from the Courts of Heaven to begin to undo the powers that control these spheres and put into place the right things of the Lord. We must also be proactive in developing reformers and commissioning them into the mountain of their calling.

Hopefully this book will help in these endeavors. Perhaps it will provide a jumping off place for thinking that could unlock a reformation into the spheres where we have influence. Whatever and however it may impact the reader, my prayer is that it helps us along the way toward this grand and awesome theme of reformation. What a great privilege and honor God has given to us to partner with Him to reclaim the earth and its societies back to His kingdom and rule. I am so grateful for the privilege. I hope you are as well. Together, let's make history and change the world.

ABOUT
ROBERT HENDERSON

Robert Henderson is a global apostolic leader who operates in revelation and impartation. His teaching empowers the body of Christ to see the hidden truths of Scripture clearly and apply them for breakthrough results. Driven by a mandate to disciple nations through writing and speaking, Robert travels extensively around the globe, teaching on the apostolic, the kingdom of God, the Seven Mountains, and most notably the Courts of Heaven. He has been married to Mary for 40 years. They have six children and five grandchildren. Together they are enjoying life in beautiful Waco, Texas.

INCREASE THE EFFECTIVENESS OF YOUR PRAYERS.

Learn how to release your destiny from Heaven's Courts!

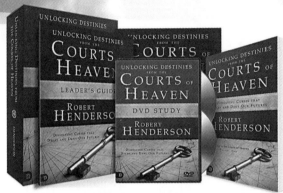

Unlocking Destinies from the Courts of Heaven

Curriculum Box Set Includes:
9 Video Teaching Sessions (2 DVD Disks), Unlocking Destinies book,
Interactive Manual, Leader's Guide

There are books in Heaven that record your destiny and purpose. Their pages describe the very reason you were placed on the Earth.

And yet, there is a war against your destiny being fulfilled. Your archenemy, the devil, knows that as you occupy your divine assignment, by default, the powers of darkness are demolished. Heaven comes to Earth as God's people fulfill their Kingdom callings!

In the *Unlocking Destinies from the Courts of Heaven* book and curriculum, Robert Henderson takes you step by step through a prophetic prayer strategy. By watching the powerful video sessions and going through the Courts of Heaven process using the interactive manual, you will learn how to dissolve the delays and hindrances to your destiny being fulfilled.

YOUR Prophetic
COMMUNITY

Are you passionate about hearing God's voice, walking with Jesus, and experiencing the power of the Holy Spirit?

Destiny Image is a community of believers with a passion for equipping and encouraging you to live the prophetic, supernatural life you were created for!

We offer a fresh helping of practical articles, dynamic podcasts, and powerful videos from respected, Spirit-empowered, Christian leaders to fuel the holy fire within you.

> **Sign up now to get awesome content delivered to your inbox**
> destinyimage.com/sign-up

 Destiny Image